POP CULTURE

W

POP CULTURE

THE CULTURE OF EVERYDAY LIFE

Shirley A. Fedorak

UTP

University of Toronto Press

LIBRARY AND ARCHIVES CANADA CATALOGUING IN PUBLICATION

Fedorak, Shirley
     Pop culture : the culture of everyday life / Shirley A. Fedorak.

Includes bibliographical references and index.
ISBN 978-1-4426-0124-6

    1. Popular culture—Textbooks. I. Title.

GN316.F43 2009   306   C2009-901881-0

We welcome comments and suggestions regarding any aspect of our publications—please feel free to contact us at news@utphighereducation.com or visit our Internet site at www.utphighereducation.com.

North America
5201 Dufferin Street
Toronto, Ontario, Canada, M3H 5T8

2250 Military Road
Tonawanda, New York, USA, 14150

ORDERS PHONE: 1-800-565-9523
ORDERS FAX: 1-800-221-9985
ORDERS EMAIL: utpbooks@utpress.utoronto.ca

UK, Ireland, and continental Europe
NBN International
Estover Road, Plymouth, PL6 7PY, UK
TEL: 44 (0) 1752 202301
FAX ORDER LINE: 44 (0) 1752 202333
enquiries@nbninternational.com

This book is printed on a paper containing 100% post-consumer fibre.

The University of Toronto Press acknowledges the financial support for its publishing activities of the Government of Canada through the Book Publishing Industry Development Program (BPIDP).

Book design: Grace Cheong, Black Eye Design

Printed and bound in Canada

Mixed Sources
Product group from well-managed forests, controlled sources and recycled wood or fiber
www.fsc.org Cert no. SW-COC-000952
© 1996 Forest Stewardship Council
FSC

To my students, who have craved a study of culture
that has meaning in their everyday lives.

CONTENTS

INTRODUCTION

The inspiration for this book germinated long before I began teaching anthropology. As an undergraduate student, I searched the calendar for anthropology courses that offered some connection, some relevance to my everyday life and reality. As a teacher, I strived to link the exotic nature of anthropology to the lives of my students by focusing on the popular culture of their generation—body art, fiction and film, music, fashion, and sports. Inspiration for this book also came from Michael Taft's ethnographic research into mock weddings in rural Saskatchewan. He taught me that we can learn as much about human nature through popular culture in our own backyard as from studying an exotic small-scale culture in some distant land.

The study of popular culture presents some interesting challenges. It demands that we, as anthropologists, look inward as well as outward, especially when examining our own society. Of equal importance is the need to finally accept that popular culture is a relevant field of study. Although kinship, social organization, and religious rituals find their way into every ethnographic study, there has been little recognition of the popular side of these activities. Indeed, until recently there has been a dearth of ethnographic information on those tangible elements of culture that make life enjoyable—folk art, games, popular music, hairstyles, and theatrics. Even today, ethnographic articles on popular culture are rare in anthropological journals, finding their way instead into some excellent books that inevitably receive harsh reviews in those same journals. The reasons for this oversight are myriad, but, simply put, academia has been notoriously afraid of the popular, and many scholars, including anthropologists, have tended to consider popular culture frivolous and shallow. Nor have they shown much movement toward a new and refreshingly open "public anthropology" that would bring topical issues, such as popular culture, to a non-specialist audience (Gottlieb 1997). Anthropologists have also tended to focus on "non-modern" people, and this has further marginalized the discipline (Asad 1993: 315). This is unfortunate because, as John Fiske (1989) maintains, culture is of everyday life. If anthropology is the study of humankind, then it must include the everyday—the popular activities that enrich our lives and give meaning to human existence. Popular culture, then, has the potential to transform anthropology into a relevant, contemporary discipline.

Several continuing themes wind their way through *Pop Culture*. Shakespeare said: "All the world's a stage, and all the men and women merely players" (*As You Like It*, Act 2, scene 7, 139–43). Throughout *Pop Culture*, popular culture as performance is emphasized. Music, art, television programs, and wedding rituals and ceremonies seem likely candidates, but the more mundane activities of our daily life, such as cooking a meal or chatting on the Internet, are also performances that convey multiple meanings and fulfill varying needs. Popular culture, then, will be viewed as a performance that shapes and is shaped by performers and audiences.

Culture is a powerful and dynamic force, constantly changing in response to internal and external forces. The processes of modernization and globalization have created many more opportunities for cultural flow, yet also raise the spectre of local popular culture becoming homogenized or hybridized, especially given the ease of communication through the Internet. Therefore, one of the central themes in *Pop Culture* will be an investigation of whether and how local popular culture is being jeopardized by modernization and globalization forces.

Identity based on gender, ethnicity, or class is also of considerable importance. The proscribed roles and restrictions that give rise to a gendered or ethnic identity, or identity based on belonging to a particular class, is explored in several chapters, most notably in popular music, body art, and wedding rituals. The concept of community finds its way into virtually every discussion in *Pop Culture*, since popular culture appears to create, sustain, and shape community. The many meanings of the concept of community are explored, as are social relationships created through popular culture. Popular culture, then, reflects, embodies, and even resists the socio-cultural patterns of human groups. Each of these characteristics is both discussed and questioned throughout this book, in particular the power to generate political and social commentary and, in its extreme forms, cultural resistance.

The themes in *Pop Culture* speak to culture as holistic and integrated, which means it is impossible to discuss popular culture without also addressing related systems of culture. Thus, connections between systems of culture and popular culture will be incorporated into our discussion.

Although this is an anthropological study of popular culture, viewed through the lens of culture, the subject of popular culture, by its very nature, crosses disciplinary boundaries into literature, sociology, history, media studies, linguistics, philosophy, art and art history, folklore, and political and economic studies. Current explorations of artistic expression and performance are interdisciplinary, collaborative approaches embracing multiple ways of knowing and understanding the world of popular culture. Therefore, the expertise of these disciplines will be drawn upon where appropriate.

The scope of popular culture is vast; the topics covered in this book were chosen in an attempt to appeal to a wide range of audiences and yet provide a glimpse into the significance of popular culture for the anthropological study of humankind. *Pop Culture* introduces students to diverse and interesting forms of popular culture that move beyond the stereotypical (e.g., pop music) into the world of virtual communities, mock weddings, and graffiti art. Yet, many worthy topics have been neglected for want of space (e.g., children's toys and games, fashion, film, memorabilia, pop fiction, retro pop culture, and countercultures). Hopefully, other anthropologists will address them in the future.

In *Part I: Introduction to Popular Culture*, the concept of popular culture and its multiple meanings, as well as the importance of popular culture in understanding human behaviour, are explored. Popular culture is not without its share of criticisms; real and perceived problems emanating from its study are addressed. This discussion is relevant in light of fears that some popular culture, particularly that found in indigenous cultures, may be threatened. To that end, globalization and media-induced homogenization of non-Western popular culture and the growing power of global youth culture will be investigated.

The role of anthropology in and the approaches anthropologists use to study culture are addressed in Chapter 2. Of increasing importance is the study of culture, including popular culture, from a performative perspective. Performance theory moves the exploration of popular culture beyond description into the analysis of how performers and audiences are shaped and shape popular culture and what they reveal about themselves through performance. An ethnographic study of Ghanaian concert parties and paintings informs this discussion. Thus, the central theme of this section is the multiple meanings of popular culture and the avenues for studying it.

Part II: Mass Media and Popular Culture is a detailed discussion of what most people readily define as popular culture—the media—in order to address the significance and meaning of performance to performers and the audience. The media serves to inform and entertain so much so that television became the number one leisure activity in the twentieth century. We will examine the impact of television on culture in Chapter 3 through the vastly popular genre of soap operas in North America and an ethnographic study of the way poor working-class Egyptian women interpret messages presented on melodramatic serials in Egypt. Popular music, perhaps the most universal of all forms of popular culture, is examined in Chapter 4. In this discussion, the ethnographic study of Afro-Cuban hip hop culture and rap music as a vehicle for cultural resistance is the focus.

Poised to become the dominant media in the twenty-first century, the Internet is a global communication system that puts information and instant contact at our fingertips. In Chapter 5, we will take an in-depth look at its power and impact. As the Internet grows in popularity, and increasing numbers of people "sign on," a new form of community has developed—the virtual community. Through the ethnographic study of an online lesbian café, we will consider the concept of community and the roles of virtual communities in creating social networks. Thus, the central theme of this section is the role of media in perpetuating, influencing, and even resisting the identity, values, ideals, and behaviour of its members.

Artistic expression is one of the universal symbols of popular culture. In *Part III: Artistic Expression and Popular Culture,* we will investigate several forms of expression found in all cultures. In Chapter 6, we will explore the many meanings of folk art and the role(s) of folk art in expressing ethnic identity, imagery, and tradition. Is street art or graffiti really art? This question is addressed first as an expression of cultural resistance among disenfranchised youth in North and South America and second as a powerful political resistance to oppression in an ethnographic study of graffiti in Palestine.

Perhaps no other form of artistic expression has garnered such attention as the ever-expanding practice of body art and adornment. Although body modification is an age-old practice, in recent years traditional beautification practices in Africa and Asia have been adopted by North Americans. In Chapter 7, we will explore the body tattoos, paintings, and piercings that are becoming increasingly popular symbols of group and individual identity, in particular the role of body art in expressing identity in the ethnographic study of prison tattoos in North America. Thus, the central theme of this section is identity and resistance through artistic expression.

The secular celebrations and gatherings of a group also give meaning to our everyday lives. In *Part IV: Gatherings as Popular Culture,* the importance of various types of gatherings on identity, familial bonds, and community is investigated. We will begin by considering ethnographic studies of the meaning and symbolism of food and dining experiences in Chapter 8, first through fast food in Japan, followed by a unique wedding ritual in rural France, known as *la rôtie*.

Nationalism is usually associated with political organization, yet popular culture plays an influential role in promoting national unity. Nowhere is this more evident than in the newly united state of Yemen where football serves as a vehicle for fostering nationalism. Sports can also be an agent for cultural imperialism or, conversely, can empower people to express cultural resistance. We will examine the place of sports in the socio-political arena, as evidenced by the role of baseball in the Dominican Republic.

Agricultural communities have always organized social gatherings to bring together isolated groups and create a sense of social bonding, as you will see in the ethnographic study of traditional Ukrainian wedding festivities. Another such gathering is the mock wedding ceremony, an often hilarious, yet culturally significant social drama enacted during wedding anniversary celebrations on the Canadian prairies. Chapter 10 will demonstrate the meanings both performers and audiences garner from these slapstick productions. Thus, the central theme of this section is the symbolism and meaning expressed at gatherings through ritual performance.

Herbert Gans (1974) has pondered the importance of popular culture in society at some length, questioning whether it is merely a commercialization of leisure activities, or whether the artefacts of popular culture—fashion, movies, and memorabilia—are cultural indicators of the values, desires, and needs of a society as they change through time. *Pop Culture* will challenge the assumption that popular culture represents the shallow end of human existence and will consider the premise that popular culture is the pulse of humankind and a mirror of cultural dynamics.

PART I

INTRODUCTION TO POPULAR CULTURE

"We have seen our popular culture and it is us."

—Browne & Browne 2001: 3.

A s the quote suggests, popular culture is the culture of our everyday lives. Human groups have always created music, folktales, festivals, and artwork in an attempt to make sense of and celebrate their world. Indeed, popular culture is a mirror of societal dynamics, it has the power to shape and reflect cultural ideals, generate resistance and activism, and represent changing social realities.

Material evidence of artistic expression and performance dates back at least 40,000 years. Thus, the artefacts of our popular culture reveal a great deal about who we are as a society and how we have changed over time. Technology, for example, has had a considerable impact, from the invention of the printing press to the proliferation of the Internet. Popular culture, then, provides tangible evidence of human interest in these issues.

Popular culture may also reveal external influences on our daily lives through the music, sports, and food that have diffused from other nations and cultural groups. Indeed, popular culture is a means of communicating the world view and circumstances of a cultural group to both its members and others. In essence, it provides an ongoing commentary on the human condition—our cherished memories, the way we live today, and our hopes and dreams for tomorrow.

In Chapter 1, we will consider popular culture and its distinguishing characteristics. If popular culture is more than just entertainment, what influence or power does it have on society, and to what degree does it reflect our societal values, ideals, and world view? Thus, we will begin with an examination of popular culture—its multiple meanings, expressions, and roles in human culture. All cultural groups possess their own forms of popular culture, yet many local popular cultures are under increasing pressure from outside forces. Will globalization eventually homogenize popular culture, especially among the youth of the world, and will this inevitably lead to the demise of local popular cultures around the world?

Popular culture is often considered superficial and without significance in the study of culture. This false impression will be debunked in Chapter 2, which discusses performance theory and the ethnographic study of Ghanaian concert parties and paintings.

Popular culture—the culture of our everyday lives—is present in all human groups and is much more than entertainment. It is the sum of performance, expression, and symbolism that both influences and reflects human culture. Its artefacts or symbols—vampire movies, graphic novels, car hood memorabilia, drums and whistles, baseball cards, patchwork quilts, banana skirts, torn blue jeans, and children's dolls—all hold meaning and, in turn, offer messages about people and their way of life. Popular culture provides shared experiences and creates the social solidarity that is the basis for all societies (Kidd 2007).

Also known as folk, common, and even public culture (Ortner 1998), popular culture is not the exclusive domain of the West; every cultural group is surrounded and immersed in its popular culture. Indeed, the American Folklife Center maintains that folk culture "is part of everyone's life. It is as constant as a ballad, as changeable as fashion trends. It is as intimate as a lullaby, and as public as a parade" (Library of Congress 2005). Popular culture, then, plays a vital role in the expression of cultural identity and the social well-being of human groups.

Cultural groups hold many elements of popular culture in common, yet each has its own set of unique customs, often influenced by other factors, such as gender, class, and ethnic divisions. The bridal shower and wedding reception are a good example of this. Although Chinese and Nuer wedding ceremonies are very different, both are steeped in customs that are part of their popular culture, and both symbolize the socioeconomic importance of joining two people and two families.

The line that determines whether an activity is popular culture or not is often blurred. Take garage sales, for example. Is "garage saling" on Saturday morning a form of popular culture? No, it is a commercial endeavour, with the goal of acquiring material goods. Yet, so is buying music or movies. Many people enjoy travelling from one garage sale to another in their neighbourhood; it is a form of entertainment, and something they anticipate all week. They meet friends at these sales and exchange news and gossip. In light of the social importance of this activity, then, yes, garage sales are a form of popular culture.

There are two schools of thought regarding popular culture: mass culture theory and populist theory (Hunter n.d.). Mass culture theory suggests that high culture—for instance, opera, classical theatre, music, and fine art—is more valuable and enlightening and that those who partake of popular culture belong to the "mindless masses" who accept and absorb it without question or critique. In other words, according to this theory, popular culture is like an opiate for the masses. The populist theory considers popular culture a vibrant pursuit that offers intrinsic and extrinsic rewards and an opportunity to escape from the stresses of everyday life. Consumers, as empowered participants or audiences, choose or reject elements of popular culture, based on their individual needs and desires. In the process, they may create a hybrid popular culture. Hybridization, the fusing together of elements from separate cultural traditions (Heaven & Tubridy 2002b), is a natural process that results from contact between cultural groups. Today, globalization and the constant migration of people, along with their culture, have increased the pace of this hybridization. Yet, well-entrenched theories of modernization and acculturation predicated on an increase in homogenization and Westernization of popular culture have not borne out in fact (Wilk 1994). Indeed, world cultures continue to generate new cultural diversities, new social and political discussions, and new forms of popular culture, while also embracing age-old practices. This suggests that although popular culture is dynamic, it is also persistent and enduring.

Despite the tendency to limit popular culture to the 1960s and onward, it has existed in one expression or another since the beginning of human interaction. Archaeologists have found chewing gum (resin), toys, and simple musical instruments in their excavations, suggesting that what we consider popular culture has been around for a very long time. Each generation modifies and makes popular culture its own, then passes it on to the next generation to continue the process.

Elements of popular culture, even if remarkably enduring, are not stagnant. Rock 'n' roll is a good example of both endurance and changeability. Although a popular and resilient music genre, Rock 'n' roll varies considerably in style and appeal, from country rock to heavy metal, glam rock to punk rock. Each type has its own fans, who may, to varying degrees, take their identity from it, often to the point of forming a microculture within mainstream society, such as the Goths have done. Thus, the type of popular culture we consume may give us our identity and separate us from other groups.

Popular culture possesses its own form of power; it can generate political commentary and activism, mirror changing social values and societal practices, resist mainstream hegemonies, and even influence the way we understand the world around us. Indeed, Combs (1984) contends that popular culture is political in that it both shapes and reflects our ideals. When the Hippies rejected mainstream society and its socio-economic structure in the 1970s, their new social order, although short-lived, became a powerful influence that is in many cases still evident today on music (psychedelic acid rock), dress (bell-bottom jeans, ponchos), and behaviour (drug use, communal living, sexual freedom, environmental awareness). Popular culture born of these countercultural movements has greatly impacted on global societies by redefining cultural institutions and challenging authority and power relations (Hunt 1999). This is particularly evident in changing attitudes toward sexual equality; legitimizing youth culture; greater social tolerance; increased civil rights for disadvantaged groups, such as First Nations or African Americans; and recognition of alternative ways of being, such as being gay or lesbian or disabled.

Rock festivals and music concerts bring together youth in a community that supports or at least considers new values and that may reject "old" sounds they consider symbolic of a repressed society (Yinger 1977). When the Soviet Union was collapsing in the late 1980s and early 1990s, Russian musicians used rock music as a vehicle for expressing their opposition to state socialism (Cushman 1995). Even something as fleeting as a television show can generate social discourse. A case in point is the immensely popular American television program, *Will and Grace* (1998), featuring the lives of several gay men and their friends. This program reflected the changing attitudes regarding homosexuality in North America at a time when the gay and lesbian rights movement was gaining momentum. Television programs like this may even serve to inform and influence people mired in misconceptions and stereotypes.

Fiske (2003: 115) claims that "popular culture is always part of power relations" and that in many ways it symbolizes a struggle to maintain a distinctive social and/or cultural identity in the face of homogenization processes. The Ukrainian-Canadian woman who continues to make traditional Ukrainian Easter eggs, a craft taught to her by her mother and grandmother, is preserving a part of her cultural heritage and identity. The same holds true of young people who adopt fashions like wearing baseball caps or baggy track suits to make a statement or who become attached to a music genre such as rap. Indeed, Daniel Miller (1995, 1998) suggests cultural consumption is replacing kinship as a cultural identity marker and that daily practices such as shopping thriftily have become acts of resistance to the establishment. In another example, some young Mexican Americans have embraced *pachuco*—the distinctive dress, loud behaviour, and language of Mexican actor German Valdez's character Tin Tan—to highlight their identity as existing within but separate from Euro-American and African-American urban culture (Durán 2002).

Popular culture may also reflect the values and issues important to its audience. This is particularly evident in the media. For example, the iconic *Star Trek* series exemplified the American way of life and by doing so promoted the righteousness of American culture in what some would suggest is an insidious form of cultural imperialism. Indeed, although the many ethnic groups and even alien cultures on board the starship *Enterprise* may appear to represent a multicultural utopia, in reality they promote the melting pot philosophy of the United States.

Popular culture has often been called the voice of the people, and these same people possess a great deal of power regarding the pervasiveness and continuity of any of its elements. Peters (2003) believes it is youth who decide what works and what does not regarding popular culture, whether it is in television, music, sports, or fashion. Widespread rejection or disinterest in a particular component may lead to its demise. This happened to North American drive-in restaurants and their rollerskating car-hops. Extremely popular gathering places for youth in the 1950s and 1960s, by the 1970s they were replaced by meeting in shopping malls. Ironically, Paco Underhill (2004) believes that shopping malls are now on the decline; young people are turning to other forms of shopping, especially online, and other places to gather, such as coffee houses, lounges, movie theatres, and virtual communities. Then again, elements of popular culture that fade away may re-emerge years later and regain their popularity as retro popular culture; this has happened particularly with many clothing styles, such as hipster bell-bottom pants.

Popular culture tends to have a more profound effect on the general public than so-called high or legitimate culture, which involves only a few people and occurs on only rare occasions. A comparison may make this point more obvious: many more people will hear a country band at their local bar than will have the opportunity to attend an opera, and many more people will read a popular romance novel than a "literary" work. According to Fabian (1978: 315), popular culture is a contemporary cultural expression of the masses that challenges notions of the superiority of "pure" or high culture.

Obviously, popular culture is linked to class: those most likely to access high culture are from the upper classes since venues for such events are expensive and elitist, while popular or common culture is more accessible to the lower and far more numerous classes. Thus, popular culture reflects social stratification and can even be used to erect and mark boundaries that keep classes within their own social spaces. Interestingly, some forms of popular culture began as high culture. The ancient practice of Japanese *kodo*—the sniffing of fragrant wood—was practiced by the upper classes. Today, aromatherapy, an offshoot of *kodo*, is enjoyed by many people. Conversely, some forms of entertainment began as popular culture and slowly lost their appeal to all but the elite. In the mid-nineteenth century, Shakespearean plays possessed "florid rhetoric, vivid characters, tempestuous gestures, and moral design" (Warner 1990: 728) that appealed to the general populace. However, by the end of that century, productions had become more restrained, and actors paid closer attention to the actual dialogue as written. As a result, the productions lost their appeal for the general public. The same happened to orchestral music, which originally provided musical extravaganzas for the working classes. When composition became more refined and experimental, the audience lost interest in the performances. This new high culture perpetuated the elitist idea that the arts should be purifying and serious, available only to the few that can appreciate it, rather than to the many who cannot understand it.

Popular culture can also eliminate or cross social barriers. The samba and tango are both of humble origins, yet are performed by people from all stations in life in all parts of the world; the only limitations are talent and ability. Brazilian dances "write their own meanings," according to Royce (2001: 541; see also Browning 1995). The samba was invented by musicians who were lower-class urban blacks, but it soon became popular with the upper classes as well, thereby crossing class boundaries and uniting a nation in their enjoyment of a musical style (Vianna 1999). The accessibility of this popular music resulted in many voices and diverse interpretations, creating multiple identities. Today, the processes of globalization and cultural flow may call into question a clear dichotomy between high and low culture as many more people gain access to such events as operas through local productions and livecast movie videos. As well, many people have become more interested and appreciative of local arts and crafts, previously considered the domain of low culture.

The influence of popular culture can be far-reaching and can set in motion new actions and considerations for its audience. A case in point is Edward Abbey's 1975 novel, *The Monkey Wrench Gang*, which inspired the environmental organization Earth First. This radical group has been responsible for numerous acts of sabotage and protest. Although it has met with societal disapproval for its drastic tactics, it has also heightened the public's awareness of environmental issues (Browne & Browne 2001). Over time environmentalism has entered mainstream society's consciousness and is no longer considered a fringe element: the twentieth anniversary of Earth Day was celebrated in 140 countries by 200 million people who took part in tree-planting, recycling, and other environmentally friendly activities (Epstein 2001). Similarly, popular music can also raise social consciousness. Canadian First Nations folksinger Buffy Sainte-Marie writes and performs protest songs that highlight the civil rights struggles of North American Aboriginal peoples, thereby increasing awareness of Aboriginal issues in mainstream society (Nagelberg 2001).

Popular culture is also quick to showcase changing attitudes toward gender equality and to influence our opinions on this topic. In television programs such as *Grey's Anatomy* (2005), strong, intelligent women hold important positions, even if they still struggle with their personal lives. These women serve as role models for other women, giving them a sense of independence and self-worth. The same can be said for literature; for example, magazines such as *Ms.* continually challenge gender norms in North American society (Kidd 2007). Nonetheless, some forms of popular culture perpetuate gender stereotypes. Dolls, for example, are children's companions, but they can also be cultural reflections of adult attitudes and values. As enculturative tools, they teach children their future roles, reinforcing prescribed gender roles, as well as perpetuating gender stereotypes. In this way, artefacts of popular culture can teach us our roles in society.

Although popular culture has been criticized for stereotyping marginalized groups or subcultures, particularly via the media (Freccero 1999), in many ways it is also a means of maintaining the traditional customs and artefacts of a subcultural group and even empowering groups to sustain their culture. For example, quilt-making is an age-old folk art that continues to thrive, has substantial cultural meaning, and remains an integral part of the Canadian Doukhobor heritage. The portrayal of quilt-making as a form of popular culture does not stereotype the Doukhobor image, it preserves it. Criticisms to the contrary, the Internet has become a boon for isolated cultural groups, such as the Inuit, to make contact with the "outside" world and enables them to inform others about their culture, thereby strengthening their cultural identity and dispelling misconceptions (Christensen 2003). Yet, the dangers of mass media and its stereotypical representations of ethnicity, gender, age, and sexuality continue to be very real and will be addressed in later chapters.

Popular Culture in the World

The effects of popular culture on people have long been debated. Most criticisms are levelled against the mass media, only one component of popular culture. It is suggested that the media's heavy emphasis on sex and violence, especially in music videos and television, has caused some people to become desensitized, skewing their sense of right and wrong. As well, feminists decry the objectification of women and human sexuality in pornography, a fringe element of popular culture. Critics also suggest that over-reliance on popular culture to entertain and occupy may inhibit the consumer's ability to appreciate higher culture.

The escapist nature of media is also considered emotionally and intellectually damaging, limiting our ability to cope with reality (Gans 1974) and turning us into passive consumers (Horkheimer & Adorno

1992). Anthropologists such as Tonkinson (2002) have seen this among indigenous cultures who are dealing with dislocation and serious socio-economic disadvantage. Contact with European settlers and dislocation from their traditional lands forced the Mardu Aborigines of Australia to resettle in small towns. This caused them serious economic problems since they lost their traditional way of making a living. Mardu youth, caught between two worlds—traditional desert life and increasing pressures from the Western world—turned not only to sex, alcohol, and gambling but to television to escape their hopeless, directionless lives. What they saw impacted on their social organization and world view, creating a whole new generation of youth who crave Western goods (Fedorak 2006).

Popular culture is often criticized for its commercial nature; its products appeal to the masses but leave little room for individualism (Gans 1974). This is a rather limited definition that focuses on popular culture as business rather than enjoyment. Certainly, some popular culture is marketed for the sole purpose of making profits, yet the same can be said of high culture: a book is for sale, whether pulp fiction or a classic literary work. The difference is in the number of people reading and enjoying it, and this is where critics use disdainful terms such as mass media. In a similar vein, popular culture has been criticized for its consumerism and its promotion of conspicuous consumption. As an example, hip hop culture and rap music, which promote resistance against the establishment, make enormous sums of money off the backs of youth who purport to reject this very consumerism.

It is also limiting to suggest that people who consume popular culture are always the victims of media manipulation (Warner 1990). Fashion is a good example of this manipulation and the actions consumers take to resist it. The fashion industry "tells" us what to wear through television and magazine ads. These norms are reinforced by celebrities who wear the clothes and stores that sell only the most current fashions, thereby directing our purchases (Kidd 2007). Although true to a point, popular fashion also includes such trends as wearing used or "retro" clothing that does little to increase the fashion industry's bottom line, and young people tend to reject clothing that they do not like regardless of what the fashion gurus are promoting. If we must criticize popular culture, and in particular Western media, for consumer manipulation, then mass marketing of Western popular culture in other cultures is where we should focus most of our attention.

Although each of these criticisms is valid to a point, it is also important to recognize that the general audience of today is more highly educated, more aware of the world outside their community, and more willing to become involved in the global community than at any other time in our history, and this is due to the media, in particular the Internet and television. Indeed, popular culture may even promote tolerance and appreciation of other entertainments and thus may perpetuate cultural pluralism (Ross 1989). Despite the plethora of what might be considered spurious entertainment, this does not appear to have had a negative impact on the audience, while the vast sources of information now available have had a predominantly positive influence. Although some forms of media may have a damaging effect on some people, this is also true of other institutions of culture, such as family, politics, belief systems, and so on.

10 Given the reach of the mass media and the Internet, as discussed above, the question has been asked, will globalization lead to the demise of local popular culture around the world? Put another way, will the globalization of media and communications result in the homogenization of popular culture and the loss of unique elements in local popular culture that are part of their cultural heritage and identity?

Cultural flow is not a new phenomenon; ideas, customs, and material objects have moved from one culture to another via trade networks, human migrations, and colonization throughout human history (Strelitz 2001). The difference today is in the speed at which this is accomplished and the volume of information (values, beliefs, and symbolic forms of popular culture) and material goods (international consumer brands) that move from one nation to another. Urbanization has also increased this process; urbanites have easier access to global fashion, music, film, and ethnic foods than their rural counterparts. In a wealthy suburb of Cairo, Egypt, a new, huge, Western-style mall features many Western brand name stores—Versace eyewear, Victoria's Secret underwear, Nike shoes, Polo golf shirts, Gucci purses. Thus, consumer brand diffusion in Egypt is well-developed despite the efforts of cultural purists within the nation to keep Western fashions out. Although these stores are a huge draw for expat youth, Egyptian upper-class youth also shop there, while to members of the lower classes fashion becomes a symbol of unattainable success.

According to Tardieu (2000), the most significant event in the process of globalization is the emergence of the popular culture industry controlled by a few Western entertainment and information multinational corporations that broadcast American popular culture around the world. Some would call this increasing monopolization and commodification of popular culture a manifestation of cultural imperialism. Indigenous folk art and crafts are in a particularly precarious position; many local crafts are lost as cheap goods flood every market economy and local craftspeople lose their livelihood. Of equal concern, popular local crafts are often being commodified to the point where their original intent and intrinsic value is lost. Apathy is also a danger to arts and crafts. As small-scale cultures are increasingly exposed to Western popular culture, young people may lose interest in their indigenous folk art. For example, Canadian First Nations quill work and bead work is disappearing because young First Nations people are not learning the craft, despite some heroic efforts to revitalize them. Yet, popular culture is flexible and often able to withstand "competition." As you will see when we consider fast food in Japan (Chapter 8), when foreign goods and services flood a market, they are often appropriated, then naturalized, until they become a part of that culture and their foreign origin is forgotten.

The influence of globalization on popular culture, therefore, is particularly noticeable among young people. According to Heaven and Tubridy (2002b), youth seem the most receptive to foreign influences and most likely to engage in the borrowing of popular culture. The power of youth culture is everywhere—from fashion trends to vehicle design, movies to television, video games to sports, and, of course, music. Advertisers recognize this power and gear their advertising to youth (Taylor 2003) and the culture industry that caters to youth needs and desires.

The overwhelming influence of Western popular culture via various media and the desire of youth in other countries to emulate North American youth have increased fears of a homogenization of popular culture and a loss of many traditional elements of local popular culture. We need look no further than Chinese weddings to witness these opposing forces. Many Chinese brides now wear Western white wedding dresses; indeed, an entire industry has developed around the desire of young Chinese brides to appear more Westernized. At the same time, these brides also wear the traditional red dress at some point in the celebration, thereby combining tradition with Western influence. The tendency here might be to suggest combining tradition with modernity; however, this is an ethnocentric perspective: white wedding dresses are not a modern version of wedding attire, they are simply a Western version.

In global youth culture "images, sounds and spectacles help produce the fabric of everyday life...providing the materials out of which people forge their very identities" (Strelitz 2001: 1; see also Kellner 1995). This powerful statement suggests both a global homogenization of popular cultures and obliteration of local popular culture under an American hegemony or a hybridization of cultural elements. If popular culture can shape as well as reflect our world views and cultural identities, as is argued here, then this new global culture may have some value. Regardless, critics label it media/cultural imperialism (Strelitz 2001), one more way to promote American values and cultural domination around the world. There is little doubt that American popular culture is having a global impact: "Kids everywhere want to be like Michael Jordan, sing like Madonna or eat at McDonalds" (Tardieu 2000: 1).

Through popular culture, people learn about other people—their values, beliefs, ideals, and patterns of behaviour. Whether this leads to a homogenization or hybridization of popular culture is open to debate, as is whether these processes are always negative. Larry Strelitz (2001) interviewed Khulani, a male student at Rhodes University from Empangeni in Kwa-Zulu Natal, Africa, who made this same point. Khulani was seldom exposed to Western popular culture until he graduated from high school and moved to Johannesburg. There, he watched television and became fascinated with the gender and familial relations depicted on the American soap opera, *Days of Our Lives.* Watching this and other programs made him aware that, unlike in his own culture, in other places women enjoyed equal status with men. He also learned that in North America children freely interact with their fathers. These concepts gave Khulani choices for how he would live his life: "I think it's sort of prepared me for my own life that I wish to live in the future when I've got my own family…so it affected me positively because when I've got my own family in the future, I will make sure that I practice those values that I find to be positive" (Strelitz 2001: 2–3).

From a North American vantage point, this change of heart is a good thing—Khulani's family will benefit from his new awareness of gender equality and familial relationships. On the other hand, these television programs have resulted in a change in his world view and a tacit acceptance of American values, which may lead to tension in his home community if he returns there. Khulani also witnessed other actions on television that he did not approve of—for example, girls as young as 15 entering into sexual relationships. He did not consider this appropriate and normal behaviour. Thus, the diffusion of ideas and behaviours through popular culture is selective; consumers will only choose those elements of a foreign culture that they find acceptable or superior to their own norms.

What this means is that members of other cultures should be given more credit for their decisions regarding what they adopt from other cultures—they can decide what to accept, what to reject, and even what to modify; this has always happened when two cultures have come into close contact. The question of homogenization and hybridization will be revisited in many ways throughout this book, but it is safe to say that well-defined, highly valued local popular culture is not going to disappear from non-Western cultures, although it may undergo some changes.

Conclusions

Simply put, popular culture is the things we do and make, the things we like, the things we believe, the things we learn, and the things we remember. It is who we are. As will become evident in the ensuing chapters, there is a great deal of diversity in popular culture, and the interconnectedness of popular culture with other elements of culture cannot be ignored. Despites numerous criticisms—over-commercialization, marginalization, skewed values, and elitist disdain—popular culture is an integral part of any culture and worthy of serious consideration. It is the key to "norm generation, boundary maintenance, ritual development, innovation, and social change" (Kidd 2007: 86).

Will Western popular culture overwhelm local popular culture now that global communications and transportation have made cultural flow so easy? The answer to this question is multifaceted. On the one hand, local cultures take great pride in traditional customs and will not easily give them up. There is a sense that they can withstand the influx of foreign influences (Tardieu 2000). Most cultures have an infinite capacity to absorb new popular culture while still holding dear their own traditional ways—the two are not mutually exclusive. If some changes occur, the new hybrid popular culture may be as intrinsically valuable as the old. Absorbing new ideas, philosophies, and behaviours enriches a culture and is a way of avoiding cultural stagnation. On the other hand, youth are fascinated with the exotic and enamoured with American popular culture; given the tendency for youth the world over to question and even reject their mainstream culture, culture loss and homogenization is a valid concern.

Will we become a global village in the hands of popular culture? The answer is unclear at this time, but Combs (1984) suggests that we may be witnessing the formation of a "common language" that unites young people everywhere who adopt a common dress, idolize the same musical icons, read the same popular novels, and watch the same movies. To that end, global youth culture may have a dramatic impact on popular cultures the world over.

There are numerous definitions of culture, but one that fits well with our examination of popular culture is "the whole way of life" (Freccero 1999: 13). This definition originates with British Marxist Raymond Williams, who considered all the practices, institutions, and thoughts of a people as part of their culture. Anthropologist Gregory Starrett (1999) has taken this further, suggesting that to remain relevant, anthropologists must expand their limited definition of culture beyond customs and traditions in order to study and understand concepts like popular culture.

If we consider culture as the whole way of life, then to ignore popular culture is to ignore a significant part of human life. Some of the resistance to studying popular culture in the West can be attributed to reluctance on the part of scholars to study the popular versions of various media: rock 'n' roll rather than symphonic music, pulp fiction rather than Shakespearean dramas, discos rather than museums. However, as Starrett (1999: 503) points out, they have also avoided "Indian dance films, Japanese hostess clubs, and Egyptian pop music." Dichotomous terms such as "highbrow" and "lowbrow" culture, "legitimate" and "illegitimate" culture, and "pure" and "mass" culture all create a perception of what is worthy and what is unworthy culture, and what is of academic interest and what is not. Levine (1988: 233) succinctly sums up this attitude: "simply because a form of expressive culture was widely accessible and highly popular it was not therefore necessarily devoid of any redeeming value or artistic merit." Popular culture, although often maligned, is "an important element in the dynamics of contemporary social life" (Kidd 2007: 81) and can be as complex and worthy of interpretation as great works of art and literature. Moreover, in part due to globalization, the boundaries between low and high culture appear to be blurring and even disappearing; take, for example, jazz music, which is difficult to categorize definitively as either high or low culture. Indeed, the study of the everyday popular culture of "the common folk" can offer interesting insights into human behaviour.

In recent decades, some anthropologists have turned to performance theory as a vehicle for studying culture. "Performance" is a broad term that encompasses many—some would say all—human activities or ritualized behaviour. In an early definition, Goffman (1959: 17) called performance "any public activity that influences other people," while Victor Turner (1986: 81) defines performance as "the presentation of self in everyday life." In this context, performance encompasses everything from complex rituals and spectacular events to mundane tasks such as preparing a meal (Bohannan 1991).

Performance theory allows anthropologists to consider a range of popular culture—from food to sports, body art to virtual communities, wedding rituals to graffiti, and music to television—where experiences, values, and symbols are presented, interpreted, and even transformed. For example, the ethnography of media enables anthropologists to follow the social players in a production, beginning with the creators and performers, who are often from other locales and of a different social class, to a diverse consuming audience (Abu-Lughod 2002b). To demonstrate these points, we will investigate how performance has fused the local and global through the ethnographic research of Michelle Gilbert on Ghanaian concert parties and the paintings that advertise these concerts. We will also discuss the various approaches inherent in socio-cultural anthropology when studying human behaviour and popular culture and how popular culture is embedded in economic circumstances, nationalism, history and heritage, human migration and cultural flow, political environment and cultural resistance, religious organization, and social relations.

Anthropological Approaches to the Study of Popular Culture

Anthropology is the study of humankind. Anthropologists seek to explain human behaviour and to understand the diverse ways people organize their lives through the lens of culture. Although they have focused historically on small-scale, non-Western cultures, today they also study the way people in modern industrialized societies live, and this, by necessity, must include those aspects of human lives that are "popular." In this way, popular culture has become a resource for understanding human cultures. This new direction has enabled anthropologists to expand their reflection on human experience and take more notice of such concepts as passion, imagination, and experience (Royce 2001), thereby opening up new and multiple methods of inquiry, analysis, and exposition.

Today, appropriation (borrowing), naturalization (making over a cultural feature as one's own), creolization (blending), power structures and barriers based on class and gender, and cultural identity and nationalism are all important concepts in contemporary anthropology. John Szwed (2005) has addressed issues of race, authenticity, and identity through the flow of popular music between cultures and the resulting creolization of music. He examined the way African Americans re-interpreted Euro-American music and culture to create black music and culture and how white Americans re-appropriated and naturalized this music, creolizing European harmonic progression with African rhythmic structures to create ragtime. Ragtime was then adapted by both the African-American and Euro-American musical communities to make it their own (Ottenheimer 2006). Interestingly, once Euro-Americans appropriated this performance style and naturalized it, its roots in African-American culture faded and disappeared—something that has also happened with rock music. Indeed, this phenomenon—losing the origins of a cultural component—has been re-enacted time and again in many areas of popular culture, including folklore and ethnic foods.

Anthropologists rely mainly on qualitative research methods to conduct their ethnographic studies: they live with the cultural group they are studying, conduct interviews with key informants or consultants, observe their daily lives, and, where appropriate, participate in their daily activities. This experiential learning, known as participant observation, enables anthropologists to develop a deeper understanding of the range of behaviours and the importance of popular culture in the community. The resultant ethnography is a descriptive, interpretive, and analytical account of their research. Maureen Mahon (2004) observed first-hand the efforts of the New York-based Black Rock Coalition (BRC) to create boundary-free rock music and reclaim its roots in black music (Ottenheimer 2006). Mahon attended meetings and concerts; conducted interviews; and collected oral histories, photographs, and written documents. At one point, she even served as secretary for the BRC. Her ethnographic research enabled her to explore the complex issues of gender, race, identity, and authenticity in this small community of musicians. She also examined their interactions with the music industry and its imposed racial and musical categories that did not fit with the reality or perspective of the musicians themselves. For example, black musicians tend to be stereotyped as soul, rap, and rhythm-and-blues performers, while "real" rock is produced by whites. According to Mahon (2004), African-American musicians have difficulty "crossing" these artificial barriers, despite the efforts of some icons, such as Jimi Hendrix, to blur racial and musical boundaries. She concluded that as whites increasingly embrace rock, they are perpetuating racial stereotypes. Yet, the stereotypes persist in black communities as well, and young African-American musicians preferring to listen to or perform rock music are mocked by their peers and face identity issues as well as racial barriers in the music world.

Anthropologists conduct their research using three interrelated approaches or perspectives: holism, cross-cultural comparison, and cultural relativism. Each culture is composed of integrated cultural systems (economic, social, political, and religious). Anthropologists must consider the influence each of these systems may have on the others. For example, popular courtship practices may be influenced or even controlled by religious beliefs; these religious beliefs may curtail or enhance the expression of popular culture during wedding celebrations. Thus, the interconnectedness of all things cultural means anthropologists take a holistic approach—they examine the culture as a whole, rather than as discrete parts. Carola Lentz (1999) compiled an anthropological and historical collection of research articles on the changing patterns of food consumption in Ecuadorian Andes, Germany, Switzerland, Zambia, Ghana, and Sudan. In these case studies gender, class, and power relations were explored in both rural and urban settings to show that "food habits are socially and culturally embedded and that any analysis of changing food habits must account for the social, cultural, and economic contexts of food" (Lentz 1999: 1037–38). This study is also an excellent example of cross-cultural comparison.

Anthropologists gather data to make generalizations about human behaviour, such as the importance of music in all cultures as a group celebration that enhances social solidarity. This cross-cultural comparative approach enables them to examine the many forms of popular culture found around the world. Hip hop culture and rap music have been compared to various forms of African music to reveal the cultural flow of style and form, as well as the importance of rap music in giving voice to the frustration of marginalized youth in many cultures. Daniel Miller (2001) explored the impact of car culture on social and cultural aspects of human lives in Norway, Sweden, Ghana, Australia, Britain, and the United States. He found that cars and car culture have transformed everyday life and were agents of change in the twentieth century. He also considered the dark side of car culture—the neglect of public transportation, the deterioration of public spaces, and the trend toward privatizing social experience, all of which have diffused to other parts of the world.

The third perspective in anthropology, cultural relativism, is a fundamental, yet contentious approach to anthropological research. Cultural relativism tries to understand a culture by examining how the people understand themselves, how they identify with their own culture and cultural traditions, and what meaning these traditions have for them. This perspective applies to popular culture as well; to view the popular culture of a cultural group without acknowledging its validity would greatly reduce anthropology and its worth as a scientific endeavour. However, considering the cultural practices of people in an objective way is not as easy as it might seem. For example, in Egypt many women wear the Egyptian *milaya*, a long loose-fitting dress, and a *hijab*, a scarf that covers their head and shoulders. This clothing conceals the woman's body and for many in the West symbolizes female oppression. But is this an accurate assessment? My own observations and discussion of this custom with Egyptian women have led me to conclude that the *milaya* and *hijab* not only provide them with a dramatic way of expressing their Muslim faith and cultural identity but for some have also become fashion statements and a symbol of modernity, especially given some of the current trends toward the colour-coordinated *hijabs* and form-fitting tunics over blue jeans that many young Egyptian women sport. Thus, religion, ethnic identity, and popular culture are all intertwined in this situation, and need to be examined objectively and from the perspective of the people practicing this custom.

Performance in Popular Culture

Humans, by their very nature, are performers. Victor Turner (1986: 81) called performance "the basic stuff of social life." Performance permeates virtually every aspect of our lives, from the mundane (cooking a meal) to the extravagant (rock concerts). Indeed, Tamara Kohn (2002: 2) suggests that "cooking and eating are performances, rich with meaning," and this meaning reveals a great deal about human culture. All performances present messages, often with multiple meanings; interpretation of these messages is determined by the cultural environment that produced the performance. The same holds true for mass media, where cultural messages abound. For example, as we will see in Chapter 3, television programs and the act of watching them hold multiple meanings for Egyptian women viewing melodramatic serials.

Johannes Fabian (1990) has urged anthropologists to shift their focus from informative to performative ethnography, moving beyond description and interpretation and into analyzing the meaning of ritualized behaviour to both the performer and the audience within the context of the group's social and cultural experience, be that historical, political, religious, or economic. Indeed, Ginsberg (1994) believes anthropologists, with their less ethnocentric perspective, their attention to productions, and interpretations of media based on cultural, social, and historical context, have much to offer the study of popular culture.

Performance theory has become a medium for investigating cultural concepts, including gender, race, sexuality, and nationalism. Beeman (1997: 2) considers performance "mimetic behaviour," meaning imitative behaviour that represents the experiences of both performers and audiences. Interestingly, the interaction between anthropologists and subjects has also been called a performance (Lamberth n.d.). Performance theory, then, allows anthropologists to study human discourse and interaction by giving them a means for considering key cultural concepts and topical issues.

Human performances are often reflexive, communicating through speech, song, dance, art, music, and so on, and thus tell much about the performers and their audience. Michael Taft's (2009) ethnographic study of mock wedding ceremonies on the Canadian prairies (see Chapter 10) illustrates this point. He looks at this ritualized behaviour within the context of everyday farm life and the issue of conflicting or dual gender roles that is communicated between performers and the audience via slapstick comedy. In the following discussion of Ghanaian concert parties, this engagement between audience and performers is also explored.

Concert parties are itinerant troupes of Ghanaian actors and musicians who perform multifaceted vaudeville acts for local audiences. The concerts offer urban popular music, stand-up comedy and slapstick, and dramatic plays (Malaquais 2001). Musicians, actors, playwrights, painters, and the audience all contribute to the production. Indeed, the temporary wooden outdoor stage is constructed in a way to avoid audience segregation and allow movement between the performers and audience. The audience, especially in rural areas, interacts freely with the performers by singing along, laughing at the jokes, weeping in tender moments, and leaping on stage to give the performers money.

Concert parties began in southern Ghana some 80 years ago and have since become a significant form of local popular culture. Bame (1981) traces their origin to year-end skits and recitations at missionary schools, while others (for instance, Collins 1976) trace them to church-organized morality plays and Bible story skits, as well as American silent films. Originally in English and held for the elite, today they are performed in the local vernacular for local people. The plays used to be two to three hours in length, but today they are all-night productions, mainly to accommodate market people without a place to sleep and to compete with lower cost entertainment like videos.

The concerts are advertised on huge plywood signboards (six by seven feet) painted with depictions of key scenes or ideas from the play. Because the paintings are street or roadside art, they are accessible to everyone, not just those who can afford newspapers. Gilbert (1998) found that although local, the paintings or cartoons as they are known locally are infused with global references from many media: folklore tales; Christian prayers and Hindu tracts; Indian, Japanese, and B-Hollywood films and videos; and events from contemporary Ghanaian life. These narrative paintings are a way to communicate and allow passersby to "read" the performance and interpret it in multiple ways.

Dramatic pictures of mythic dwarves, forest giants, vampires, and monsters (like King Kong) permeate the paintings alongside biblical imagery. This imagery is transformative: "to portray the tiny mischievous forest spirits with backward feet of Akan folklore called *mmotia*, he [the artist] transforms the bearded dwarves from illustrated European children's fairy tales" (Gilbert 2000: 6). In the paintings for the play *Have Faith in God,* a crucifixion scene is balanced by the depiction of a prehistoric animal. This form of hybrid imagery both represents and communicates the rapid changes taking place in Ghanaian society. Global images become part of the local via the cartoons and the play they represent, and the scenes juxtapose the everyday lives of Ghanaians with the supernatural. According to Gilbert (1998: 63), "To understand the painting one must examine the way in which the images responded to local expectations, address specific local situations, and draw upon popular music, local folktales, prophetic Christian churches, TV shows, sign-paintings and paintings on the backs of lorries, and local clothing styles."

The all-night concerts begin with extensive introductions of the musicians by name and town of origin. Their rural origins are stressed, thereby linking them socially with the audience. As many as 40 musical numbers are performed along with sexually suggestive dancing, interspersed with comedy, including ethnic jokes, puns, word games, and humorous stories, all relevant to Ghanaian popular culture. This entertainment reaches the audience in some emotional way, such as by singing the song *Maame,* which is dedicated to everyone's mother (Gilbert 1998: 77). This is known as copyright time—the musicians are playing other people's music. They then perform some of their own compositions, again interspersed with ethnic jokes and advice for the audience on how to live good lives.

The culmination of the concert is a dramatic play, described by Gilbert (2000: 1) as "a multi-act that combines vaudeville, morality drama and Christian revivalist sermon" that often lasts until dawn. The concert plays are morality tales addressing local concerns, such as competition and jealousy in polygynous marriages, fear of sorcery, the importance of ancestors, fragmentation of the extended family, underemployment of urban youth, poverty, and conflicts between traditional religions and Christianity (Malaquais 2001). Although the messages are generally androcentric, these plays are seldom politically or sexually subversive; they are more an attempt to convince the audience to give up their evil ways by eliciting a particular response or performance from them.

Originally all the performers in a concert play were men, with three stock characters: the joker, the gentleman, and the "lady" (Collins 1994). Today, stock characters also include a lineage elder, Queen Mother, chief, spirit medium, Islamic *mallam,* and a Christian priest. Dressed in strange clothing and make-up, the joker/trickster is responsible for the narrative. During the play, *Adowa* songs from the Akan ethnic group, Akan funeral dirges, Christian hymns, and "highlife" tunes are all performed. Highlife music, which originated in the 1920s, is a dynamic creolization of several music genres: *osibisaba* rhythms of the Fante people of southern

Ghana, Caribbean *kaiso*, Western foxtrots, Liberian *dagomba*, the *ashiko* and *goombe* of Sierra Leone, and Congolese guitar riffs and dance music (Malaquais 2001).

Like the paintings, the plays also take their form from diverse sources: early twentieth-century Akan tales of Ananse, a trickster figure; nativity plays from Christian missionaries; and Hollywood movies, American vaudeville acts, and "blackface" minstrel shows. Their imagery has been heavily influenced by foreign films, especially horror and science fiction films, such as *Jurassic Park* (1993) and prehistoric cavemen movies. Many of the plays depict the living dead (mummies), monsters (Godzilla), zoo- **21** morphic creatures (a three-eyed bull dog with a human body), local gods, and Satan. Sources are as wide-ranging as the Michael Jackson *Thriller* video, Japanese television serials, Indian musical films, Nigerian horror/ morality videos, and such Christian iconography as angels bearing swords. These foreign videos and religious symbols introduce a global aspect to the concert plays.

Thus, the plays are reflections on contemporary Ghanaian life and, as such, provide commentary on both the uneasy co-existence of Christian, Islamic, and traditional religious practices consistent with chieftaincies and the struggle between church and state. They have offered timely political commentary: in the 1940s they addressed World War II; in the 1950s and 1960s, independence struggles; and in the 1970s, government corruption. Westernization and colonialism figured heavily in those decades. By the 1990s there was little political commentary, although the reasons why this is so remain unclear; it is perhaps due to changing tastes or political censorship. The 1990s were also the time when concert parties became televised and sanitized entertainment, featuring domestic conflicts more than monsters. In the last decades of the twentieth century, much of the material for the concert plays was drawn from Apostolic Christian prayer groups who encouraged people to become Christians.

Attendance at concert parties appears to be drawn along class lines. Less educated, rural, and impoverished youth make up the majority of the audience, perhaps because they are in closer touch with many of the images depicted. "When members of such an audience see a tree stump portrayed on a brightly painted board they know it represents an *obosom* [traditional god]..." (Gilbert 1998: 81). Children living in urban centres and attending Christian schools are less aware of these traditional beliefs, and the concerts are less meaningful for them. Concert plays are stigmatized by the elite who openly express their disdain for the concert parties and the audiences who attend them. On the other hand, the concert parties and audience acknowledge this contempt and defuse the power of the elite by making fun of their own lack of status and couth, thereby using the performances to contest these stereotypes and to resist the dominant class.

Concert plays are morality plays with verbal, musical, and visual representation that offer commentary and discourse on contemporary cultural, social, religious, and political issues important to Ghanaian people. In these plays, good triumphs over evil, providing the audience with hope for salvation and a return of social order. These concerts and paintings also offer the performers and the audience an opportunity to reflect on the reality of their lives, something that Gilbert (1998: 84) calls collective reflection. Ultimately, the concerts and the cartoons depicting them link the local and global, the present and past, the mythic and the everyday (Malaquais 2001).

Conclusions

According to Beeman (1997: 12), "Performance is the means—perhaps the principal means—through which people come to understand their world, reinforce their view of it and transform it on both small scale and large scale." The performative approach suggests that actors through performance reveal much about themselves, and the audience through observation and participation also learns about itself. In this way, studying performance helps us to understand human culture.

The study of popular culture enables anthropologists to identify and track global changing patterns of human culture. According to some theorists, these patterns of change are articulated through the various elements of performance—the performers, audience, situation, setting, and cultural context (Magoulick n.d.). The interdisciplinary nature of performative theory challenges traditional disciplinary boundaries, bringing together gender studies, history, political science, and culture studies to study cultural issues, such as race, gender, identity, sexuality, social or countermovements, economics, and political issues. Anthropologists have embraced performance theory to understand the dynamics of cultural groups through their performance behaviour.

Although little direct reference to popular culture is made in performance theory, the production and consumption of popular art, fiction, music, and food, as well as celebrations, are all part of the human experience and, therefore, performances. As we have seen in the Ghanaian concert parties, popular culture provides insightful commentary on contemporary issues that are important to all human cultures.

22

PART II

MASS MEDIA AND POPULAR CULTURE

Although popular culture comes in many guises, it is the media that predominates. Popular media, also known as mass media, not only entertains, it also informs, and may even shape audience perceptions and understandings of the world. The media can also reflect the values, interests, and concerns of viewers. The power to both shape and reflect the world view of performer and audience will be a major consideration in the next three chapters. There is little doubt that media is an agent of change, and as North American popular culture has spread to other regions of the world, it has impacted on local popular culture; we will investigate to what degree this has occurred and whether this represents cultural imperialism.

Questions pivotal to this section are: to what extent do media—television, music, and the Internet—shape the audience's world view, or is the media merely a reflection of already formed views? Is the audience a passive receptor, or do viewers play a role in shaping the type of media and the messages the media will send? Is media an agent of cultural imperialism and the eventual homogenization of a global popular culture? To answer these questions, we will explore the ways in which people transmit and receive diverse messages through performance and how performance mirrors issues important to both performers and audience.

Considerable research on media, especially television, has been conducted by researchers in various fields of study. However, mass media, with its label of "pop" culture, appears to have prevented anthropologists from considering it a meaningful contributor to the study of culture and society. Indeed, Debra Spitulnik (1993: 293) has lamented "there is as yet no 'anthropology of mass media.'" Kottak (1990) believes that anthropologists have ignored television because of their hesitation to become involved in studying modern societies and because of their distaste for any instrument that might reduce cultural diversity. Sherry Ortner (1995) calls this resistance "ethnographic refusal." However, as anthropologists have increasingly encountered television, radio, and even the Internet in the cultures they study, they have come to realize that media is diffusing to virtually every corner of the world, that it is becoming part of people's everyday lives, and that its messages are absorbed, interpreted, and even resisted to varying degrees among these cultural groups. Research into the economic, political, and cultural flow from urban to rural locales and Western nations to developing nations is also becoming increasingly significant. Thus, popular media can no longer be ignored by anthropologists as a means of social expression (Armbrust 1996).

Armbrust (1996) demonstrates the importance of anthropological research into popular culture in his investigation of the role media has played in creating a national sense of modernity in Egypt and how this sense has changed over the course of the twentieth century. He found that between the 1920s and 1960s, "modern" education became a focal point of the Egyptian working class as they embraced Western images of a comfortable middle-class life that ran counter to the country's conservative intelligentsia. By the 1970s, the dream had faded as Egyptians faced the reality of a deteriorating economy and infrastructure, and the educated masses woke up to a lack of jobs and economic opportunities. Serial television programs that reflected this reality became popular, in a way resisting the dysfunction and corruption of the Egyptian elite. Egyptian mass media in the 1990s no longer promoted idealism; rather, programming increasingly contested the exploitation of the poor by upper-class Egyptians. In a similar vein, Abu-Lughod's (2002b) ethnographic research on the impact of melodramatic serials on poor Egyptian women will be a major focus of Chapter 3.

Chapter 4 examines music as popular culture, a study that has long interested anthropologists, although attending to popular music such as rap is in its infancy. From an anthropological perspective, music is set within the social context of society, as musical style links to cultural patterns and social processes (Turino 2007). For example, J. Duany (1984) studied Puerto Rican salsa by examining the historical development of popular music within the context of socio-economic trends in the country. He also considered the social function and symbolism within salsa and explored what the music meant to the people of Puerto Rico. John Szwed (1970: 220) reminds us that "song forms and performances are themselves models of social behaviour that reflect strategies of adaptation to human and natural environments." Thus, music creates and recreates cultural values, similar to folk legends, celebrations, and clothing fashions. In other words, popular music synthesizes the elements of a cultural group's ethos.

Anthropologists have examined the processes of appropriation, naturalization, and creolization of music to create new genres. For example, the Euro-American dance team of Vernon and Irene Castle took creolized (blended) African-American dance styles and turned them into ostensibly white ballroom dancing (Ottenheimer 2006). As another example, "called" dances, such as African-American quadrilles, were creolized into square dances and redefined as a white dance. Hence, the roots of African-American dance traditions have been "lost." This categorization of dance and music (e.g., rap and soul as black) is a continuing process that has little connection with historical facts and everything to do with racial politics. Hence, authenticity is also an important issue in the anthropological examination of music and dance.

Academic publications, such as the *Journal of Musical Anthropology of the Mediterranean*, speak to the vibrant research being conducted in some regions of the world. For example, questions of ethnicity and identity have occupied ethnomusicologists in Turkey where so-called minorities (Armenians, Jews, Greeks, Kurds, Laz, Arabs, Georgians, and Roma) contribute substantially to Turkish musical life and impact on Turkish identity (Stokes 2006). Yet, there are serious gaps in the study of music and dance. Potuoğlu-Cook (2006) laments the lack of research on belly dancing in Turkey—a fact he credits to the ostracized label of "popular" for the art form—and there is a similar problem in the neglect of popular music in North America.

Anthropology's late foray into cyberspace means that little attention has been paid to developing theoretical or practical approaches to the study, and few ethnographic studies of the Internet have been conducted. There has also been little anthropological investigation of the Internet's impact on cultural groups, in particular indigenous groups now thrust into the technological age. Yet, the Internet and cyberspace are slowly attracting the attention of anthropologists. Several recent case studies of Internet use illustrate the broad range of research possibilities online; for example, Wheeler (2003) studied how Kuwaiti women use the Internet for political action, while Clark (1998) examined American teenage dating practices through chat rooms.

Chapter 5 will look at the Internet and virtual communities as popular cultures. Wilson and Peterson (2002) have suggested that anthropology is uniquely suited for the study of virtual communities because of its cross-cultural, multilevel approach. To that end, they have begun to examine emerging online communities, positing that online socialization and practices must be studied within the context of existing physical and social realities in everyday life. Anthropology can offer a unique perspective on how gendered and racialized identities are negotiated online. Indeed, a new specialization known as cyberanthropology examines humans interacting in networked environments and is gaining momentum within the discipline.

In the 1950s, television burst into North American homes and became "a magical doorway into images and experiences that both nurtured and stretched the limits" (Toerpe 2001: 441). Television crossed cultural and national boundaries, offering audiences a vast range of visions and experiences beyond their local communities, and by the 1980s it had become the most popular and influential medium in the world. Television programming has expanded considerably since those first snowy sporadic pictures and today brings dramas, comedies, documentaries, music, sports, and news to diverse audiences. In a 1986 *TV Guide* survey, 68 per cent of American people chose watching television over food, liquor, sex, vacations, money, or religion as their favourite pastime (Kottak 1990). It continues to grow in popularity and influence in most regions of the world, and according to D'Acci (2004: 374), television has become a major "social, economic, cultural, and ideological institution."

The ongoing debate regarding the impact of television on culture, including popular culture, poses some interesting questions. Just how much influence does television have on its audience? Are these audiences merely passive recipients of whatever message producers decide to broadcast, or do they interpret messages and accept or reject them based on their own life experiences? Does television influence our desire for consumer goods and change our social relationships and social behaviour? Or is it merely a reflection of well-entrenched values and behaviours? What is the impact of Western television programming on local popular culture?

Television audiences have been accused of passively absorbing whatever programming comes their way. Although there is some merit to this accusation, audiences are neither as passive nor as pliable as some critics suggest. In this chapter we will investigate the impact of television on its audiences through the ethnographic research of anthropologist Lila Abu-Lughod (2002b). She has studied the way Egyptian women from lower socio-economic classes interpret messages embedded in Egyptian melodramatic serials and examines whether the goal of "educating" Egyptians about what it means to be a modern citizen through such programs has been successful.

The Impact of Television

Conrad Phillip Kottak (1990) considers the impact of television on human society to be at a comparable level to kinship, religion, political organization, and education. He also suggests that television is actively creating new experiences for its audiences, thereby generating new meanings. Television has increased cultural awareness by bringing the beliefs, ideals, and patterns of behaviour of other cultures into our homes. Whether this creates a better understanding of other ways of thinking and being is open to debate. Nevertheless, people are now more aware of the world outside their community than ever before. This is partly due to television.

For some time, people inside and outside academia have been voicing their concerns about the impact of television on viewers. Indeed, the film *The Running Man* (1987) even spoofed television's manipulation of its audience. Contempt has been heaped on the medium as an intellectual wasteland mired in crass commercialism. The heavy emphasis on violence and sexual content has given rise to dire predictions that watching television may lead to moral decay and interfere with more productive pursuits, such as reading great works of literature. These fears have led some to question the wisdom of allowing television into their homes. However, Newcomb and Hirsch (2000) point out that most of the criticisms levelled against television also apply to other media, including literary works.

Educational programming in the guise of popular culture is a good example of the positive influence television can offer. Jim Hensen created a world populated by half-marionette, half-puppet creatures—the muppets—that exhibited human personalities and behaviours. In 1969, *Sesame Street,* an experimental children's show peopled with Hensen's anthropomorphic muppets, came on the air, and nearly 40 years later it is still the most widely viewed and beloved children's program in the world. It is watched in more than 100 countries, each in a foreign language version relevant to that culture (Jackson 2001). Despite a few nitpicking criticisms over the years, it continues to be a mainstay of children's programming and has become a model for "edutainment"—educational entertainment—programming. *Sesame Street,* then, is the epitome of a popular culture icon brought to us through television.

The impact of television on cultures outside the West is of considerable interest. Indeed, cultural "protectors" worry about the influence of Western television and whether it is an agent of cultural imperialism and homogenization of local culture (Richards & French 2000). When people from other cultures tune into American television by satellite, they witness an unfamiliar world that appears consumed with material wealth, violence, and sexual activities. This exposure cannot help but have an effect on and may have some influence on cultural diversity. The Mayan people of Guatemala managed to maintain a great deal of their popular or folk culture for a thousand years, yet with the advent of television and radio, Mayan peasants are increasingly turning to the outside world and forsaking their traditional culture (Shuman 1991). In the near future this irreversible trend will likely have a profound effect on their cultural systems. As a further example, the rooftops of Egyptian apartment buildings are covered with satellite dishes; although Egyptian families enjoy Arabic programs, they also have access to American and British programming that defies many of the cultural mores (modest clothing) and values (women's roles, traditional family) of Egyptian society. How this exposure is affecting young Egyptians and their view of the world around them is of increasing concern to parents and Muslim leaders alike.

Researchers have found that audiences in developing countries relatively recently exposed to television are not being homogenized as much as feared. Rather, as you will see with the Egyptian case study below, people tend to prefer local programming and only accept themes that resonate with their own cultural experiences, thus mediating these outside influences. This is evident in mainland China where the most popular programs are those deemed relevant to Chinese society. Although American shows such as *Desperate Housewives* (2004) are very popular, one of the most well-watched shows is actually Korean, a reflection of the enormous cultural influence Korea has in China. *Big Changjin* is the story of a woman, Xu Changjin, who lived in the Korean Palace 200 years ago. Although Xu Changjin dreamed of becoming a chef to the emperor, she became involved in palace intrigue, was enslaved, and sent away. While away she earned her medical licence and then returned to the palace to face her accusers. Her skills earned her the position of emperor's physician and the title of Big Changjin at a time when Korean women were not allowed to work as men's doctors. The program features Korean food, which is extremely popular in China, and Xu Changjin's virtuousness is deeply admired.

There are numerous examples of television actually enhancing cultural identity. When television first arrived in northern Canada in the 1970s, Inuit people were inundated with CBC programming that had little to do with their lives. The Inuit Tapirisat, the national political organization for Inuit peoples, lobbied for their own programming, which became a reality in 1991 when a satellite-delivered Aboriginal distribution system was established (Meadows 1996). TV Northern Canada serves 100 communities in French, English, and 12 Aboriginal languages. Produced on their own terms, Inuit programming, such as narratives of their history, has enhanced Inuit culture and even served as a means of political mobilization. Many other indigenous groups have recognized the efficacy of using media to further their political, economic, and cultural aims and, in so doing, have created a "mobilization of identity" (Ginsberg, Abu-Lughod, & Larkin 2002: 9). They use mass media to document traditional activities, offer language literacy programs, advertise their political struggles, communicate with dispersed kin, use video as legal documentation during negotiations with states, create public awareness of their presence and issues, and produce award-winning films (Abu-Lughod 2002a: 10).

Television, as well as other media, has served to strengthen national identity. In Hong Kong, television created a local Cantonese-based cultural identity that distinguishes the island from mainland China. Television producers in Hong Kong accomplished this feat by developing distinct programming and promoting local entertainers who have become popular cultural icons. These measures created a sense of social solidarity among Hong Kong citizens.

Daytime television is different than evening programming in both audience and content. Generally, the audience is comprised of retired people, stay-at-home mothers, and others who do not work outside the home. The content is designed to touch on personal issues that would be of interest to this audience. Indeed, it could be claimed that daytime programming deals with the everyday far more than evening programming does. One of the most popular forms of daytime television is the soap opera, a continuing daytime drama known as *telenovelas* in Latin America and as melodrama serials in other parts of the world.

How many people regularly watch soap operas? This is an innocent enough question, but when posed in my anthropology classes, it created momentary confusion and a sense of discomfort that was amusing to observe. A few self-confident students raised their hands immediately; others looked around uncertainly to see if anyone was responding, then tentatively raised their hands halfway, hoping that only I would notice. Still others shifted in their chairs, laughed self-consciously, and refused to look up. Only after listing my favourite soaps and linking the plotlines to something in our discussion (such as the use of body language) did they realize that it is acceptable to admit to such a "vice." In my experience, males seem more hesitant to admit to watching soap operas than females. Gillespie (2003) found that many young men are keen viewers of the Australian soap *Neighbours* (1985–07), although they do not talk about it. This behaviour is consistent with the less than stellar reputation of soap operas and the fear that admitting to watching them could cast aspersions on one's intelligence, sophistication, and productivity.

Soap operas generally focus on domestic themes of home and family, love and betrayal—albeit in a fantasy world of money and opportunity—and emphasize emotions and affairs of the heart. Some are character-driven, while others are issue-driven, but all are essentially narratives about contemporary life. Oftentimes North American soaps reflect a "Cinderella" storyline: working-class people become rich by some means, only to trade one set of problems for another. These stories are similar to folktales: ordinary people are faced with extraordinary problems that are brought into their safe little community by "outsiders." On the other hand, British soaps are based on social messages that draw attention to the contributions working-class people have made to their country; since the so-called American dream of rags to riches is not valued or even believed, it is not portrayed. On the British soap *Coronation Street* (which has been on the air since 1960), the storylines have an element of idealized nostalgia for the past, especially for World War II. This era has taken on an almost mythical aura, and the soap's characters are the epitome of the "strength under fire" British wartime mentality (Anger 1999: 123). China's daytime soaps revolve around the Qing dynasty, and the shows are alive with kung fu, magic, palace intrigue, and elaborate costumes. They reflect nostalgia for earlier times as the country becomes increasingly modernized.

Although often maligned and relegated to second-class entertainment by critics, soap operas serve to inform the audience as well as to entertain them. They have broken through social barriers, dealing with issues such as abortion and homosexuality, and they regularly address domestic violence, child abuse, racism, alcoholism, drug abuse, sexual harassment, and interracial marriages. This programming both reflects and influences traditional institutions, such as marriage and the family. In China, Confucianism and strict laws made divorce uncommon in the past, but with today's mobile and affluent society, couples are able to get quick and simple divorces. This social dynamic is explored on the popular television show *The Chinese Divorce*, which follows the lives of three couples from marriage to divorce. Soap operas also provide valuable information on medical problems, such as breast cancer and AIDS, eating disorders, and mental illness (Pulliam 2001). These are the everyday problems of everyday people.

Why, then, are soaps so disparaged? According to Anger (1999), soap operas deal with domestic issues and romance, which are considered the realm of women and, as such, possess a lower status than other programs geared toward male interests. Television critics ignore soaps, regarding them as trash. Anger draws an interesting parallel between the television critic's reluctance to analyze soap operas and the academic's unwillingness to analyze popular culture—both refuse to recognize the social and cultural significance of these media. This contempt for soap operas also maligns the audience. Soap opera fans are stereotyped as lazy, unemployed, unintelligent women with nothing better to do. Obviously, there is an element of gender discrimination in this attitude. Soaps are viewed as a woman's genre and, therefore, not as worthy as men's escapist entertainment, such as sports. Even feminist scholars have shown a disdain for soaps and soap fans, contending that the characters and storylines of soaps stereotype women and their lives by mainly focusing on issues of home and heart.

Why, then, are soaps so popular? The answer to this question is multifaceted. To some, soaps are "company," a way to occupy an hour in an otherwise mundane day. This is part of the reason soaps are so disparaged—only bored or boring people watch them. This, of course, is untrue; people from all walks of life and socio-economic circumstances watch soap operas. Soaps are also an avenue for social bonding in that discussing the storyline draws people together for "soap chats" that may enhance friendships and contact with family members. In Australia, soap chats are known as "soap gossip" and amount to a form of socialization among friends as they discuss characters and plotlines (Gillespie 2003). Recounting the stories on a soap opera during soap chats is a form of storytelling. Anger (1999) even likens long-term soap viewers to keepers of the "family" history; they are the equivalent of "griots," the keepers of tribal history in traditional African societies. Soap chats become a shared experience that may even entice non-viewers to begin watching the shows in order to participate in this form of socializing both online and on coffee row. In essence, soap watching becomes a daily ritual and brings some constancy into viewers' lives (Williams 2001).

Soap operas, like other genres of television, may increase social solidarity. *Telenovelas* are Brazilian melodramatic serial fiction very similar to North American soap operas, although they differ in that there is eventually a conclusion to the serialized story. Originally, *telenovelas* ran for 15 to 30 episodes before resolution, but today they may run for more than 100 episodes. Kottak (1990) suggests that watching *telenovelas* creates a social solidarity among the audience that is comparable to the solidarity gained from religious worship and may even contribute to the creation of a pan-Brazilian national culture, since every night 60 to 80 million Brazilians watch the commercial network, *TV Globo*, which produces its own shows. Brazilian television emphasizes the importance of the extended family, and most shows take place in domestic spaces, tackling difficult social issues, such as racial divides, gay and lesbian relationships, and gender equality. Recent *telenovelas* have centred on "bureaucratic corruption, single motherhood, and the environment" (Aufderheide 1993).

The enormous popularity of Latino *telenovelas* has diffused to North American television. *Ugly Betty* (2006), the story of a young woman working at *Mode*, a high fashion magazine, is based on the Colombian *telenovela*, *Yo Soy Betty La Fea*. The phenomenal popularity of this show may be due to the violence, corruption, and drug culture endemic in Colombia. Betty, by contrast, has become symbolic of the innocent and uncorrupt. Betty is neither thin nor beautiful, which means she represents normal people, unlike the fashion models and TV stars more commonly seen on television, and she deals with the same embarrassments, inequalities, and hassles that normal people experience in their everyday lives (Soong 2001).

In the 1990s, anthropologist Lila Abu-Lughod conducted television ethnography in Egypt. She asked if there was any relationship between television and the processes of modernity and what impact, if any, Egyptian television had on its audience. In a study of the impact of melodrama serials on Egyptian women, Abu-Lughod (2002b) focused on two female demographic groups: poor working-class women domestics in Cairo and rural women in Upper Egypt villages. She investigated the contrast between intended messages and the way the audiences actually interpreted these messages.

Television was first introduced to Egypt in the 1960s, although an unreliable infrastructure (lack of electricity) and widespread poverty put TV sets out of the reach of most Egyptians until the 1970s. Television opened the world to Egyptians, a vast majority of whom are illiterate, and brought the non-local into their homes. Of particular note, television offered women, the young, and rural people the same access to the outside world that was previously available only to urban men. Today, television is an icon of popular culture in Egypt; to own a colour television is a sign of status and modernity for many Egyptians, while a lack of familiarity with television is synonymous with rural backwardness and symbolizes typical urban contempt for peasants in Upper Egypt. Television, then, equals modernity.

Despite opening the world to Egyptian audiences in the 1980s, television was mainly a state-controlled agent of propaganda. It was used by urban, middle-class professionals in the culture industry to "enlighten" and modernize the lower class citizens of Egypt (Abu-Lughod 2002b). The peasant class was the targeted audience since it was the largest demographic with the lowest income and standard of living. Since melodramatic serials are Egypt's most popular television genre, they were an excellent mechanism for educating the lower classes. They provided directed narrative to encourage education in what Abu-Lughod (2002a) calls "development realism" to put Egypt on the path to modernity. There was resistance to this pressured emotion; many saw through the propaganda when, after sacrificing a great deal for their children's education, they found there were few jobs for them and little improvement in their standard of living.

Government officials and the intelligentsia were out of touch with the common people. They failed to recognize that television is only a small part of the complex daily lives of the lower classes and that Egyptians are faced with other agencies bombarding them with competing messages—multinational corporations advertising Western-style products;

Islamic groups demanding religious loyalty; and an elite that is increasingly turning to the West and, in the process, becoming Westernized. Despite their good intentions, these serials denigrated Egyptian peasants and their customs as backward, seeming to suggest that educated urban producers were modern and enlightened and knew better what Egyptians must do to improve their lives. Thus, television became a major instrument for transmission of social and political messages, as well as a focus for resentment and cultural resistance.

As has been discovered in other regions of the world (i.e., India), interpretation of program content is influenced by the events and circumstances of the audience (Abu-Lughod 1997). For example, in the popular Egyptian melodrama *Hilmiyya Nights,* female characters exemplify the dilemmas faced by many Egyptian women in the conflict between their traditional and modern roles. Older women characters are mistreated by their husbands and must deal with secret marriages and other deceptions. Younger women struggle with conflicting emotions regarding career and marriage. The serial also promoted a glorified and unrealistic vision, exhorting the values of education beyond the possibilities for most people. For example, in one highly unlikely scenario, the daughter of a coffee shop owner and a singer became a university professor.

Abu-Lughod (2002b) found that the Cairo domestic workers she studied ignored the political and social messages of the serial and focused instead on the charismatic characters, such as Nasik Hanem, an aristocratic, conniving femme fatale, who dressed in beautiful clothes, and Hamdiyya, a belly-dancer. One informant said, "Nazik is the reason everyone watches *Hilmiyya Nights.* She's tough; she married four men. She wouldn't let anyone tell her what to do." The women were fascinated by a character who lives a glamorous life they could never attain and who displays personality characteristics and behaviour, such as controlling a man, they could never emulate. This is similar to North American viewers who watch soap operas to see "how the other half lives."

In *Hilmiyya Nights,* Nazik and Hamdiyya defied Egyptian moral and behavioural conventions but also fell from grace. Nazik could not accept that she was growing older, and she was swindled out of her fortune by her fourth husband, a much younger man. To camouflage her age, she wore a wig over her grey hair and clothes designed for younger women; moreover, she sought the company of a 20-year-old man. Derided for her unbecoming behaviour, Nazik had a nervous breakdown. Hamdiyya, too, had problems, becoming addicted to heroin and losing everything. Despite their glamour, these two characters dealt with the same problems as other women in Egyptian society: ageing, dishonourable men, and poverty. However, none of the informants mentioned the moral lessons in the serial. Instead, they were intrigued by Nazik's defiance of the moral system that insists on women being "good." This message resonated with women domestic workers who struggle with the shame of having to work outside the home as servants, which calls into question their respectability and status in the community. Since the 1980s, to appear modern and urbane, women have dressed in Islamic style (Abu-Lughod 1997), so, in an attempt to counter their humiliation, many of these working-class women have adopted the *hijab* (head scarf) as a symbol of middle-class respectability, modesty, and Islamic piety.

The political messages in the serials were also ignored by all but one of Abu-Lughod's informants, who mentioned that the drama was "against Sadat," that it showed what happened with the *infitah*, and that it warned against imported foreign "putrid" food like canned meat (Abu-Lughod 2002b: 316). It was evident that most of the women did not watch the serials to learn what to think. They were selective in the messages they interpreted and ignored aspects that were not part of their life experiences. They only acknowledged and accepted moral messages that fit with their lives and world view, such as the importance of family and a mother's role. For example, one informant commented on the unhappiness of Nazik's daughter, Zohra: "The poor thing. It was because her mother didn't take care of her.... Zohra never knew the love of a mother...." (Abu-Lughod 2002b: 317).

Every household in the village Abu-Lughod studied near Luxor had a television set, most of them black and white with poor reception. Only the wealthiest families had colour sets. Most evenings the television was on, unless there had been a death or illness in the family. Like the poor working-class women in Cairo, the villagers also resisted messages that did not fit with their lives. The impact of serials like *Hilmiyya Nights*, with their urban settings and upper-class problems, was minimal because the plot and characters were so far removed from the everyday realities of women who live in mud-brick two-storey houses with wooden doors wide enough for donkeys, sheep, and water buffalo to pass through to the pens inside. The stories, although entertaining, had little to do with a village life mired in poverty, hard labour in the fields to harvest enough clover for livestock, and raising families in a rural setting. When watching the serials, the women focused on such family dynamics as divorces, arguments, absent spouses or children, and match-making, which were familiar problems. Yet, many of the "women's issues" dealt with in the serials—men unable to commit to marriage for fear of losing their freedom, mothers upset because their children were not emotionally open to them, and psychiatrists treating drug addiction in the wealthy—were foreign to these women.

The kind of modernity the Egyptian serials depict is upper-class life, where educational and employment opportunities are easily accessible.

This differs from the life experiences and modernity of rural peasants who worry about poverty, underemployment, ill health, police corruption, pollution, and religious nationalism (Abu-Lughod 2002b: 322). Even when a serial supposedly reflecting village life was written (*Harvest of Love*), the villagers rejected it, adamant that problems like revenge killings did not happen in their village (they did); they simply did not see the connection between the drama and their daily lives.

Ultimately, Egyptian women are fascinated with the melodramatic serials, yet there is little doubt in their minds that these fictional stories are outside the realm of their experience and therefore do not significantly affect their world view. The storylines and characters portray different problems, they follow different rules, and they are not part of the local moral community. Television, then, at least for the Egyptian women in Abu-Lughod's study, is just one aspect of their lives, and the processes of modernity promoted in the serials have had little impact on their attitudes or experiences.

Conclusions

Without a doubt, television has changed the human experience, bringing new images and events to people the world over. In the twenty-first century, television has become a national and international medium, responding to pivotal moments in history; creating public forums; and calling on audiences to laugh, cry, get angry, change or expand their minds, and join together in social solidarity. The daily ritual of tuning into *Coronation Street, Hilmiyya Nights, The Tonight Show, Lost,* or the *NFL* can create a sense of shared experience and community.

Television is much more than an entertainment medium. It is a forum for expressing ideas, values, and cultural mores. In 50 some years, television has become an integral component of human society, an influence as powerful as family, peers, religion, and schools. It can create an international sense of sorrow through images of tragedy (the 9/11 terrorist attacks, the death of Princess Diana, and the political and natural disasters of Hurricane Katrina and the tsunami in Indonesia) or galvanize us into becoming involved in protecting the environment or righting civil injustices. Once in a while, television even inspires its audience, in portraying such events as the 1969 American landing on the moon or the 1989 fall of the Berlin Wall. Television, then, is a powerful enculturative force. Indeed, it can not only be a hegemonic mechanism for imposing the values, beliefs, and practices of a dominant society onto others but it can also preserve, validate, and express local cultural identity.

Despite a tendency to search for deep meanings in soap operas, they are first and foremost popular entertainment. The process of watching and discussing the soaps with fellow viewers is a socially shared experience that creates bonds and may in some way help viewers deal with their daily lives. Soap operas present universal stories of star-crossed lovers, family relationships, and community issues set within a particular time and place. Thus, they are an increasingly recognized form of popular culture, found in many regions of the world. As with television in other countries, the content and style of Egyptian television has changed over time in response to the economic, political, religious, and social circumstances of the nation, yet it continues to emphasize what is important to Egyptians and has served, to varying degrees of success, as an instrument for social development and modernization (Abu-Lughod 2002b).

D'Acci (2004: 373) believes that television gives its watchers "a sense of who and what they are, where they are, and when (morning, late-night, holiday seasons…), if they are safe or in danger (from threatening weather, hostile attacks, economic recessions…), and how they ought to feel and be." Simply put, television plays a role in how people think about themselves and the world around them. Although this discussion has emphasized the power of television to influence its audience, we must never forget the ability of people to think for themselves and to reject messages that do not resonate with their lives. Media may introduce the topics, but audiences determine whether they are worth exploring.

Music in some form or another is a universal pattern of human behaviour. Everyday life is reflected in the songs and dances, chants and raps that people hold dear. Popular music, in keeping with our definition of popular culture, is music that people have access to, can participate in, and enjoy on a regular basis. Music and dance produce multiple meanings, communicated through multiple channels that are interpreted in multiple ways by both the performers and the audience (Royce 2001). Abenaki music is a good example of this: Abenaki shamans used cedar flutes to call game, lure enemies, and attract women (Stokes 1992). Music, then, can be a reflection of a culture's values, ideals, and patterns of behaviour, while also providing commentary on social, political, economic, and religious issues.

Whether a particular style of music is part of a group's popular culture is sometimes difficult to determine, especially since it is used for many purposes: religious ritual (although some religious sects, like the Amish, forbid music), political commentary, nationalism, economic reward, seduction, and, of course, celebration. Popular music overlaps other genres; for example, some Christmas carols have become so popular and commonplace that they can be considered popular, not solely religious music.

Music genres do not exist in isolation, and, like television, popular music transcends cultural and social boundaries. Contemporary North American popular music is heavily influenced by Cajun, Yiddish, and African music. African tribal music combined with Celtic folk music to produce the blues, country western, and rock 'n' roll (Rosendorf 2000), and elements of African-American rhythms are embedded in not only hip hop but are also heard in contemporary Lakota performances of ancient courtship songs (Stock 1996).

The wide variety of African music and dance available in most North American cities is a testament to the rich heritage of African immigrants. In metropolitan Washington, African immigrant music includes "popular dance music such as Zairian *soukous* (influenced by Cuban rumba), Cameroonian *makossa* (Douala area jazzy, rumba influence), *shaabi* (working-class music) from Egypt and Morocco, and Nigerian highlife" (Dompere & Fadopé 1997). The reciprocal flow of musical styles is evident in Trinidadian steel bands, which are a compilation of African and Hispanic music combined with British and French influences. Conversely, music genres such as hip hop are becoming popular in other regions of the world at an incredible rate. Young people are listening to hip hop music on their iPods or other electronic equipment in countries like Kenya (Taylor 2003). In Egypt, I have observed the little basket boy stationed outside my apartment building listening to American hip hop and rock 'n' roll on headphones he must have borrowed from someone. Children and youth the world over now have access to technology that brings them popular music and videos, regardless of their socio-economic circumstances or geographic isolation.

Obviously, popular music should be studied within its social, historical, and cultural context. In this discussion we will consider questions such as the role popular music plays in revitalizing, expressing, and maintaining identity. Popular music has had a profound impact on youth culture around the world; as Frith (1992: 177) states: "Music is not just something young people like and do. It is in many respects the model for their involvement in culture." Using hip hop culture and rap music, we will consider the roles music plays in social and political commentary and how that music has become a vehicle for cultural resistance.

Defining Music as Popular Culture

Did humans first create music in an effort to imitate bird calls? Were Neanderthals able to fashion simple musical instruments for their enjoyment? When was the first song performed and why? These are difficult questions to answer. Some of the earliest evidence of music comes from China where a multi-note flute dated to 8,000 years ago was discovered. Tomb paintings depict ancient Egyptians and Sumerians playing reed flutes. Even more amazing, archaeologists have discovered ancient bone flutes and whistles, including a bone flute found in western Slovenia, dated to 43,000 years ago (Turk 2003). Certainly, contemporary hunter-gatherers possess a vast array of music and musical instruments that are ancient in origin.

The connection between cultural, political, spiritual, and popular aspects of music is evident in many forms of ethnic music. Calypso music originated in the eastern Caribbean and is rooted in traditions brought to the New World by West African slaves mixed with European influences. This music is a reflection of Afro-Caribbean working-class identity, but it also provides a platform for satire, protest, and defiance of colonial presence (Lockard 2001). As such, colonial governments considered calypso music subversive and tried to suppress it; however, its popularity continued to grow, even to the point of gaining international recognition.

Thus, popular music, like all other forms of popular culture, is embedded in the systems of culture. This interrelatedness affords anthropologists a glimpse into the way people interpret their world, their history, and what is important to them.

Music, including popular music, serves many purposes. Popular music can be used to announce important rites of passage such as childbirth, puberty, weddings, and funerals. Wedding songs are an integral part of folklore in the Middle East (Rosenhouse 2003). Men and women may sing the songs as solos or they may sing in groups. Even though they come from Christian, Druze, Muslim, and Jewish cultural groups, the basic elements of the songs transcend religious and communal boundaries. The same can be said of the polka, originally a Czech peasant dance from Eastern Bohemia in the 1830s (Peterson 2001), which evolved into myriad styles; today, many ethnic groups claim the polka as their own. Songs can also be used to maintain peace and tranquility in a community. During Inuit song duels, each performer tries to outshine the other with dance-songs and drumming; in this way they settle disputes and vent anger without appearing angry, since showing emotions is not approved of in many Inuit groups (National Geographic Society 2006).

Popular music affirms and celebrates cultural identity. With the fall of the socialist regime in Mongolia in 1990, the country enjoyed a renaissance of what Carole Pegg (2001) calls "Old Mongolia." The performance of this music symbolizes ethnicity, origins, heroes of the past, and a new nationalist commitment. Thus, identity is created and recognized by both the performers and audience (Pegg 2001: 8). Mongolian music has been undergoing a post-socialist hybridization as it has been appropriated for commercial use in the West, a practice decried by Pegg. Nonetheless, diverse Mongolian identities are celebrated through their performance art (Bulag 2003). The music is also representative of tensions between ethnic groups and questions a true national unity.

Popular music influences and reflects social mores, as is the case with square dancing. In the United States, President Reagan designated square dancing the country's national folk dance (Peterson 2001). Square dancing is more than an entertaining physical activity and avenue for socializing, it is also a code of conduct: the ten commandments of square dancing advocate friendliness, acting one's age, cleanliness, prohibition of smoking and drinking alcohol, a dress code, and traditional gender roles.

No discussion of world music would be complete without an examination of throat singing, which involves producing two or more notes simultaneously (Sklar, n.d.). Throat singing is found in several cultural groups around the world, including Tibetans, Mongolians, the Ainu of Japan, and Chukchi of Siberia. It often mimics animal sounds or other sounds in nature. Shamans in Asia invoke the spirits using throat singing.

Inuit throat singing (*katajjaq*) is a rhythmic game mothers play with their children during the long winter months. Often two Inuit women will face each other and have a contest to see who can out-perform the other, which amuses the children. In recent years there has been a resurgence of interest in throat singing among some Inuit peoples, and the same can be seen in the larger population, where more people are learning this intricate form of singing.

Work songs were a common form of folk music used in the past to coordinate difficult or dangerous work, pass the time, and relieve tedium. The *ghinnáwa* "little songs" of the Awlad'Ali Bedouin punctuate conversation between women as they make bread and perform other daily chores. Besides whiling away the work day, these songs address personal issues, such as sexuality, that would be taboo during normal conversation but within songs is acceptable. In Vietnam, work songs are called *ho*, meaning to "raise the voice" (Stock 1996). These songs match the rhythm and pattern of manual work.

Making music can become a coping mechanism for marginalized groups, a way to express dissatisfaction and make their grievances known. Protest songs, like the anti-war protest songs written and performed by American musicians Joan Baez and Bob Dylan during the Vietnam War era, provide political commentary, spread ideas, and raise issues concerning civil and human rights. When migrant workers moved from rural areas into Tunis, they brought with them *mizwid*, played on traditional Tunisian bagpipes, a genre of music that quickly became popular throughout the country. *Mizwid* has often been described as Tunisian rap music; it is a musical expression of the disenfranchised. The socially elite scorn this music because it is associated with lower-class, marginalized people (Stapley 2006).

On the other hand, music may also be used to manipulate cultural groups politically. The Turkish government, intent on gaining acceptance in the European Union, tried to ban *arabesk* music (Stokes 1992), which began in Istanbul in 1979 and quickly became popular. *Arabesk* is Arab-derived music that gives voice to the disenchantment and alienation many youth feel in Turkish society. As with other forms of popular music around the world, the elite disdainfully labelled *arabesk* decadent music. In essence, it is the voice of Turkish counterculture and reflects the enormous upheavals Turkish society has experienced in the twentieth century. *Arabesk* music, then, highlights a common theme in popular music—alienation, marginality, and disenfranchisement, whether among youths, ethnic minorities, migrants, or the poor. Both of these actions—political protest and political manipulation—are evident in hip hop culture and rap music.

Hip hop culture and rap music began in the mid 1970s as a local expression of New York inner city youth, mostly African Americans, West

Indians, and Latinos, and has become a major countercultural force in popular music globally; today rap is rocking the casbah, the ghetto, and even cyberspace (Best & Kellner 1999). Like rock 'n' roll, hip hop culture goes beyond a musical style (rap and deejaying) to encompassing visual art (graffiti and street art), fashion (baggy pants) b-boy/b-girl(ing) (breakdancing) and a distinctive language, attitude, and lifestyle. As the popularity of hip hop grew among youth, so did the popularity of the lifestyle. Yet, hip hop culture is constantly changing, absorbing rhythm-and-blues (R&B), funk, soul, reggae, techno, pop, and house, then creolizing the music to create new styles. One of its elements, break-dancing, originated in the Bronx in the mid-1970s (Powers 2001). It was an urban street movement until 1983 when the movie *Flashdance* propelled the art onto the international scene and moved hip hop culture into mainstream consciousness.

Rap music is one of the most significant and influential aspects of hip hop cultural expression. The first wave of rap was intimately connected to African-American popular music, from the nationalist fervour of *Zulu Nation,* to the racial politics of *Public Enemy* and feminism of Queen Latifah, to the ghetto experience of Grandmaster Flash. In early hip hop, DJs isolated percussion breaks in funk music, and MCs urged the audience to dance with rants between songs and later began speaking over the songs. Since then, rap has influenced other musical styles and culture, essentially breaking down boundaries between music, imagery, spectacle, and everyday life, and in the process creating a new technoculture (Best & Kellner 1999). Within a historical and political context, rap gained most of its popularity during the Reagan-Bush (Sr.) era when African Americans experienced enormous hardships as wealth was shifted away from them, welfare programs were cut back, and the concerns of the poor were ignored.

Thus, as a powerful forum for cultural and political expression among disenfranchised youth, rap addresses issues of race, police violence, drug abuse, and sexism, which, at the very least, has resulted in an increased awareness of these problems (Best & Kellner 1999). Although heavily criticized and censored for its lyrics and content, rap music at its most controversial level is a form of protest song. According to ethnographers Best and Kellner (1999: n.p.):

> Rap is thus the voice and sound of hip hop culture while dance and bodily movement enact its rhythms and moves; graffiti inscribes spatial identity and presence, and fashion provides subcultural style; music videos present a compendia of hip hop's sounds and images; and digitized multimedia furnish a sign of its migration into new cultural terrains and the next millennium. Encompassing

style, fashion, and attitude, hip hop culture ethos becomes a way of living, a genuine subculture and way of life, appropriate for the postmodern adventure.

Imagery is everything in hip hop and rap. Some rappers cultivate the rebel or outlaw image through the clothes they wear and their behaviour, while others use political rap or what has been called "conscious rap" to represent themselves as "knowledge warriors" and spokespeople for the marginalized and oppressed. Still others project a range of Afrocentric black nationalist sentiments that includes cool and funky urban hedonism. Rap music, then, is about identity and self-assertion. In their music, rap artists make clear "who she or he is, where they are from (e.g., the hood or ghetto), what time it is now (time of intense poverty) and what is happening (rebellion, uprising)" (Best & Kellner 1999: 7). It provides a distinctive language, style, and attitude. At its best, rap brings attention to and denounces racism, oppression, and violence. It also celebrates black culture and pride. At its worst, rap is racist, sexist, tends to glorify violence, and has become so commodified that much of its power and sincerity have disappeared.

Youth use rap as an expression of their disgruntlement and alienation from the establishment. In essence, rap performers facilitate conversations between the disenfranchised and those in power. Youth the world over have responded to its rhythms and rebellious tone. Brett Lashua (2006), in his ethnographic study of rap music among First Nations youth in Canada, found that rap lyrics offered considerable insights into the political issues youth were facing: problems in northern reserves, racism, disintegration of their cultural and familial ties, the need for informed and relevant education, poverty, drug and alcohol abuse, and police violence.

In her study of the relationship of Afro-Cuban rap music with the Cuban socialist state during a time of increasing racial disparity and economic crisis, Sujatha Fernandes (2003) addressed the multiple meanings of hip hop culture and rap music. Fernandes conducted her ethnographic, historical, and semiotic study of cultural resistance and appropriation in Havana, Cuba, between the years 1999 and 2002. She found that the hip hop movement and rap music began in earnest in 1994 with pioneer rap groups SBS, Primera Base, Triple A, Al Corte, and Amenaza leading the way. American rap music was appropriated, creolized, and naturalized by Cuban rappers, yet Cuban rap is distinct from both Cuban oral traditions and American rap. Artistically, Cuban rap has its own style and has enjoyed growing levels of support within and outside Cuba. Like African-American rap, Cuban rap is protest music; the lyrics raise issues of race in Cuba and challenge and contest the official racial blindness of the state.

When the Soviet Union collapsed in 1989, economic depression threatened the viability of the Cuban state, necessitating drastic measures. Programs of self-sufficiency in food, wide-scale rationing, and heavy reliance on currency from foreign tourism impacted on Afro-Cuban youth, who watched their opportunities for economic self-sufficiency disappear. As conditions worsened, racial inequalities, prejudices, and stereotypes became increasingly visible, and racial conflict and restricted opportunities for Afro-Cuban youth created hardship within the community. State policies of austerity and legalization of American currency divided Cuban society into those with access to and those without resources. It is within this historical-political framework that "rap music has taken on a more politically assertive and radical stance as the voice of black Cuban youth" (Fernandes 2003: 580).

Rappers use their lyrics, style, and performance to address racial stereotypes and to project an image of fear and machismo that throws these stereotypes back in the face of those who perpetuate them. In her study of African-American youth, Trisha Rose (1994: 12) suggests this is a mechanism of self-defense: "The ghetto badman posture-performance is a protective shell against real unyielding and harsh social policies and physical environments." To a certain extent this applies also to Afro-Cuban youth who tend to be harassed by the police and labelled criminals and drug dealers by mainstream Cubans.

The hip hop movement in Cuba is not homogenous. Two types of rappers have emerged: underground and commercial. Underground rappers, like Los Paisanos, are similar to North American "conscious" rappers who promote cultural resistance and who link black activism to hip hop culture. This black militancy appeals to Cuban youth who increasingly feel the effects of racial discrimination. Through their lyrics, Cuban rappers defy state policy by identifying with their race, criticizing racial injustice, challenging national stereotypes of Afro-Cubans as criminals and delinquents, addressing the repercussions of slavery in contemporary times, and demanding inclusion of marginalized Afro-Cubans in the political and economic discourse of their country. Their lyrics are political messages that only reach limited audiences of like-minded people. According to Fernandez (2002), underground rap groups maintain a radical stance close to the origins of the genre and avoid commercialization. Indeed, they are often hostile toward commercial groups who have "sold out," offering only diluted political messages that perpetuate Cuban stereotypes of mulatta women, rum, and cigars.

Commercial rappers, like Orisha, seek popularity and financial success. They incorporate popular Cuban rhythms to increase their authenticity and to become commercially viable to large audiences (Fernandez 2002). If fortunate, they sign contracts with transnational record producers;

indeed, many Cuban rappers embrace a "fantasy of wealth" similar to American rappers, although their chances of financial success are far more limited. Sales count more than message for many commercial rap groups, although most Cuban commercial rappers, who blend salsa and other instrument forms into their rap music, are not commercial successes, and their musical styles are really artistic choices.

Commercial rappers also promote alternative strategies, such as hustling and consumerism, for marginalized Afro-Cuban youth to make a living and resist the state's ideals of morality. Street hustlers befriend foreigners for money and gifts, sometimes through sexual favours, sometimes through thievery and trickery. This behaviour works outside the Cuban socialist government's labour control, contradicts socialist ideology and morality, and siphons off money from the state. Nonetheless, it persists. Ultimately, both commercial and underground rappers are using their music to contest racial inequalities and lack of opportunities for black Cuban youth.

Fernandes (2003) argues that although rap music can be used to voice discontent over socio-political conditions, it may also be drawn into the agenda of the dominant group and may even reinforce the hegemony of postcolonial nation states. For instance, Cuban state officials originally promoted the commercial rap music of groups like SBS because they were popular, their lyrics contained nothing dangerous to the state, they made people dance, and their style diluted the radical potential of rap (Fernandez 2000). As well, global marketing of the music brought in money from foreigners and increased revenue-earning potential. However, the state became increasingly drawn to underground rappers because of their rejection of American commercialism and because they had become a very powerful voice among Cuban youth. The calls in underground rap music for equality and justice echoed the messages of Cuban leaders. Their images of rebellion and resistance appealed to Cuban hegemonic strategies, since in many ways the Cuban nation is itself an underground resistance movement rebelling against neoliberalism and struggling to promote socialism. Thus, rap music was appropriated by the Cuban state to foster national cohesiveness, create a transnational image conducive to foreign investment, and regain popularity with its own citizenry.

Appropriation of the underground message by the state to serve its goals calls into question globalization theories that suggest cultural flows endanger nation-states (Appadurai 1990) and that unfamiliar lifestyles broadcast on international television will overwhelm local politics (Gilroy 1987). These theories ignore potential alliances between transnational and national bodies. In this case, Cuban rappers are building networks with African-American rappers based on race and marginality that transcend any national borders while also generating a critique of global capitalism that allows them to collaborate with the Cuban socialist state (Fernandes 2003).

Collaboration with the Cuban state allows underground rappers greater visibility and diffusion of their messages while facilitating increasing acceptance by political leaders that racial discrimination does exist in Cuban society. Indeed, the Cuban Minister of Culture has admitted, "We are supporting this movement because the message of Cuban rap profoundly reflects our contradictions, the problems of our society, the theme of racial discrimination, and it strongly highlights the dramas of marginalized barrios" (Fernandes 2003: 597). Hence, the state is giving more institutional support to rap music, coordinating yearly rap festivals and enterprises that support a range of music genres; in turn, the rappers help to maintain the Cuban state's hegemony. There is a downside to this support; it also means that underground rappers have lost some of their autonomy. In spite of this, rappers participate in multiple networks of African-American rap and the global music industry enables them to resist some aspects of state co-optation and maintain some of their autonomy. Nonetheless, a relationship of dependency threatens. Commercial rap, on the other hand, has not been appropriated by the Cuban state, because its consumerism and individuality does not fit with the socialist ideal. Yet, the Cuban state recognizes its potential for revenue and enhanced tourism, by which the state may maintain its social structures and fund institutions such as schools and hospitals.

The hip hop movement in Cuba reflects trends in American hip hop, such as conspicuous consumption: wearing designer label clothing like Tommy Hilfiger, as well as the baggy pants, sweatshirts, and baseball and stocking caps that are all gestures of defiance against the dominant society. Cuban rap audiences use their clothing and American slang ("mothafuka") to distinguish themselves as a group and to highlight their identity as Afro-Cuban youth. In a way they are attempting to break down barriers by dressing like the "enemy." Adopting hip hop clothing is also a way for Afro-Cuban youth to exhibit their cross-national identification and collective sense of black identity. Female rappers, such as Obsesion and Instinto, also project alternative images of women by wearing African gowns or long baggy shirts and pants, thereby establishing a non-sexualized style to challenge the stereotype of scantily dressed Tropicana dancers represented in Cuban popular culture.

Cuban rappers have devised multiple strategies for expressing their needs and desires, and the hip hop movement is a new vehicle for Afro-Cuban youth to express their individuality. Fernandes demonstrates that the hip hop movement is diverse, with multiple voices and multiple meanings and associations. Cuban rappers have combined the "politics of race, style, consumerism, nationalism, and anti-capitalism into a multi-faceted movement that reinforces local and global forms of power, while also providing a voice of resistance" (Fernandes 2003: 603).

The role of rap music in Cuba demonstrates how cultural producers negotiate power relations. Cuban rappers have contested emerging racial hierarchies, demanded social justice and a voice in Cuban politics, and promoted alternative strategies for survival, such as hustling and consumerism. Yet, as we have seen, there is also conflict in Cuban rap between commercial success and such resistance.

Hip hop culture is a fusion of activism, consumerism, style, and cel- ebration of black culture. This means that rap music, indeed all rap, cannot be linked to any one political agenda. Fernandes (2003) reached three conclusions based on her ethnographic research. First, Cuban youth have appropriated rap music to contest the Cuban state, raise issues of racial discrimination and social injustice, and develop strategies for economic survival outside the norm. Second, the socialist Cuban state has harnessed the creative energy of Cuban underground rappers to maintain its dominance despite increasing social instability. Third, Cuban rappers participating in transnational networks of record companies and African-American rap have options that prevent their total co-optation by the Cuban state, meaning that they maintain a degree of autonomy. Fernandes's findings challenge the theory that globalization of commerce and cross-national solidarities based on race and ethnicity leads to the undermining of national sovereignty.

Conclusions

In this chapter, we have focused on the roles popular music can play in society and its efficacy in cultural expression and resistance. Keeping in mind that popular music is the music of everyday life, we see that it: 1) is a vehicle for reflecting a culture's values, ideals, and history; 2) revitalizes and celebrates cultural and national identity, and cultural continuity; 3) provides a medium for socialization, be that a grandiose concert or a small family celebration; 4) provides a forum for social, political, economic, and religious commentary; 5) empowers youth subcultures and provides them with an identity and a tool for cultural resistance to state hegemony; 6) bridges the gap between ethnic groups; 7) provides opportunities for transnational and transgenerational discourse; 8) provides an avenue for state manipulation of the citizenry, such as by inciting nationalistic sentiments; 9) spins-off new fads and behaviours that keep society vibrant; and 10) entertains.

Music is symbolic communication that gives meaning to the history, traditions, and world view of a cultural group and enables others, such as anthropologists, to interpret their world. Popular music is a powerful and emotive means of maintaining and expressing identity in cultures around the world. For youth, it appears to provide an identity; nowhere is this more evident than in the rap music that has become embedded in youth culture.

Although hip hop has been criticized for becoming clichéd, over-commercialized, and a tired music genre, in Cuba, Brazil, Columbia, and Venezuela, as well as some African countries, it is drawn upon to raise local issues of race and marginality. Therefore, "rap music provides an avenue for contestation and negotiation" (Fernandes 2003: 584).

Popular music is both a reflection of cultural mores and a way to empower members of a culture to express their gendered and ethnic identity, to uphold their world view, and to resist inequality. Popular music, then, provides a medium for social and political commentary. Whether a genre of music is considered popular is sometimes difficult to determine; in the end, if people enjoy the music and it has meaning for them, then it is popular, regardless of genre or status.

48

"Reach out and touch the world."

The quote may sound like just another clever advertising slogan, but for millions of people connected to the Internet, it has become a reality. Internet traffic has doubled annually since the early 1990s (Wilson & Peterson 2002), and estimates suggest that over one billion people used it worldwide in 2006—a 200 per cent increase since 2000 (Internet World Stats 2006). The degree to which the Internet has impacted individuals and groups, and the way in which it has transformed our lives, is still hotly debated, but there is little doubt that it has become embedded in people's daily routines. Indeed, Franklin (2001: 1) calls going online "an emerging practice of everyday life," and on November 15, 2006, *Good Morning America* named the Internet one of the seven wonders of the modern world.

The American military created the Internet in the 1960s to decentralize and prevent a wide-scale shut down of their communication systems; Scott (1998) facetiously calls the early Internet a war toy. In the 1970s, university scientists and college communities adopted the technology to facilitate their research projects. By the 1980s, personal computers had found their way into private households, and the Internet quickly attracted the public's attention. In the ensuing decades, the Internet changed the very nature of global communications. Its social impact is equivalent to how telephones and automobiles freed people from the physical confines of their communities in the early twentieth century.

The Internet and its role in popular culture cannot be viewed in isolation; it is influenced by many cultural elements, including socio-economic status, gender, and cultural and national identity. The Internet, in turn, impacts on popular social interaction (through online media, for instance), acquisition of information (previews of television programs and films, graphic novels), economic activity (cybershopping), political discourse (gay and lesbian cafés), and the flow of popular culture (online gaming, music). Howard, Rainie, and Jones (2002: 71) believe that for Americans, at least, "use of the Internet tracks with the rhythms of their lives at work and at home."

In the early years of the Internet, a digital divide separated users from non-users. Age, gender, ethnic identity, socio-economic status, and geographic location (that is, whether one was living in a developed or developing country, rural or urban area) all determined whether individuals accessed the Internet and the degree to which it affected their daily lives. People with lower socio-economic status and less education, women, and those who were older tended not to use computers or the Internet as much (Jensen 2001). By far the most obvious digital divide was between North America and the rest of the world, with the poor in developing countries at the bottom of this hierarchy (Chen, Boase, & Wellman n.d.). The gender gap is more pronounced in South Asia, Latin America, and Eastern Europe, where less than 30 per cent of women have access to online communication. The typical Internet user in the early 1990s was a young, white, North American, urban male with a fairly high income and education level (Chayko 2003).

Of considerable concern is the ease with which the Internet may become an instrument of Western cultural imperialism, affecting the popular culture of other societies. There is little doubt that it is having an impact on global popular culture, especially youth popular culture; however, the extent to which popular culture is changing because of it remains unclear. Kim (1998), rejecting suggestions that information on the Internet is controlled by Westerners, suggests that it has assisted in the flow of cultural and other information in many directions; some scholars even suggest that it is diluting the Western elite's previous monopoly on information. Ezines are an example of this cultural flow. Ezines are online publications that appeal to individuals who see themselves as somewhat marginalized (Scott 1998). Ezines reach people around the world, providing poetry and prose fiction; forums for political ideologies and self-exploration like body image, sexuality, and relationships—what Rheingold (1995) calls participatory democracy. The Internet facilitates a broader and more immediate circulation of these publications, which often have chat rooms attached to them, and a form of reciprocal exchange, where the publishers can hear from the readership. Despite the Internet becoming a powerful mechanism for sharing popular culture, the jury is still out on whether it is also an agent of cultural imperialism.

How is the Internet relevant to our discussion of popular culture? Is it even accurate to consider the Internet to be popular culture? These questions may generate considerable debate among readers, but if we define popular culture as the culture of our everyday lives, then the Internet has become not only a vehicle for popular culture but also a form of popular culture itself. In this chapter we will explore some of the ways in which the Internet has impacted on socialization, with a brief look at a Japanese senior citizens' online group. The concept of community has been called into question with the advent of so-called virtual communities. We will consider community as social space through the ethnographic research of Shelley Correll (1995) into a lesbian bulletin board known as the Lesbian Café.

The Internet and Community

Although critics lament the amount of time people spend in front of their computers, particularly youth playing online computer games, even they have had to admit that the world has grown smaller and people have become less provincial because of the Internet. This Information Super Highway has expanded our awareness of other people and other ways of living and in its own way has fostered understanding and respect between groups of people through their shared experiences "online." The Internet has also facilitated the sharing of popular culture on a global level. Music, art, hobbies, sports, and special interests are all within easy reach and generate considerable political and social commentary.

Inuit people in isolated communities in the Canadian Arctic have embraced the Internet as a tool for strengthening their community and sharing their culture with the outside world (Earthwatch n.d.). Youth use the Internet to communicate with widespread friends and family and to introduce other students to their Inuit culture, including their popular culture, while adults use it to advertise their crafts and promote ecotourism. Thus, the Internet has become a part of Inuit everyday life, and through it they are building new cultural bonds and sharing their popular culture with the southern world.

Our ability to communicate with a wide network of friends and family, and even strangers, has been profoundly affected by the Internet. In the Howard, Rainie, and Jones (2002) study, nearly 60 per cent of the respondents reported an increase in their communication with friends and family with the advent of e-mail. Bulletin boards, e-mail, chat rooms, and instant messaging have all facilitated the sharing of common interests and enhanced socializing between "cyberfriends." In a survey of Netville, a suburb near Toronto, Canada, researchers found that wired households enjoyed significantly more informal contact with their neighbours than non-wired residents (Wellman et al. (2003). They also maintained more long-distance connections with family and friends, which enabled them to continue their extended support network. The researchers labelled this phenomenon glocalization, which they define as a combination of local and distant social relationships, in this case via the Internet. The newest manner of wired communication is blogging, a type of personal journal that enables users to share their thoughts, ideas, and life experiences with people around the world. The Internet has also created electronic diasporas that link dispersed participants. This connection has enabled families to stay in closer contact, strengthened familial ties, and helped sustain the traditional and popular culture of diasporic communities.

Howard, Rainie, and Jones (2002) investigated the role the Internet played in the everyday life of several types of users: netizens, utilitarians, experimenters, and newcomers. The most avid users are "netizens," who fully incorporate the Internet into their daily lives for work and play. They e-mail and blog, shop online, do their banking, and enjoy various online hobbies. Thus, for netizens, the Internet provides easier, quicker access to popular culture. "Utilitarians" approach the Internet with a functional aim (online banking); "experimenters" try out new activities online (blogging); and "newcomers" tentatively use various fun features, such as e-mailing a friend.

Critics suggest that computers and the Internet may increase social isolation (Nie & Erbring 2000). They fear that people who previously spent part of each day with friends will now remain at home, playing games, surfing the "Net," immersing themselves in commercial pages (like eBay), or becoming mesmerized by unhealthy and illegal pastimes, such as gambling and pornography. Yet, Howard, Rainie, and Jones (2002) found most Internet users decreased the amount of time they spent in other solo activities, such as watching television, to make up for their time online and tend not to reduce the amount of time they spend in personal or telephone socializing with friends. Indeed, they found that e-mail enhanced social networks and encouraged a camaraderie that is very similar to face-to-face friendships. In fact, face-to-face may become a moot or at least confusing point since web-camming allows people to see each other as they communicate on the Internet, and services such as IM (Instant Messaging) allow participants to hear each other.

Many people use the Internet to construct social relationships in cyberspace. Teens find chat rooms a less threatening environment than the "real" world, according to Subrahmanyan, Greenfield, and Tynes (2004). The teens in this study used chat rooms to discuss their concerns about sexuality and to exchange identity information in order to facilitate "pairing off." This is true in many regions of the world. For example, Kuwaiti youth turn to the Internet in the evenings for social contact, unlike their parents and grandparents who gather at someone's home or the local *diwaniyya* (male social clubs) (Al-Mazeedi & Ibrahim 1998). The Internet offers a way to avoid gender boundaries otherwise strictly enforced in Kuwaiti society, thereby creating a sense of gender autonomy. Yet, these gender restrictions are still somewhat evident in cyberspace—what is "decent" behaviour for

52

women online is hotly debated by men and women, young and old alike (Wheeler 2003).

The Internet also crosses sectarian lines—in Kuwait, Shi'i and Sunni belong to the same virtual communities and chat rooms. Thus, the Internet offers a sense of being one with the world, which may provide some freedom from cultural restrictions. All of this has created concern among more conservative Kuwaiti adults, who fear that this introduction to new ideas will counter traditional cultural and religious teachings and sow discontent among the young. Moral codes may be subverted and thus create a contradiction of identity. Cyberdating, in particular, has caused a great deal of concern in cultures where families traditionally choose a spouse for their children. Despite these concerns, the Internet has become an integral part of Kuwaiti youth subculture as a leisure activity and a way to avoid gender restrictions. They use the Internet as a medium for cultural resistance on a limited basis and, at the very least, as a challenge to pre-existing value systems.

53

The Virtual Community

Millions of people on every continent participate in computer-mediated social groupings known as virtual communities, a term coined by Howard Rheingold (1993) to identify computerized networks of widely dispersed individuals sharing common interests. Virtual communities are cultural aggregates that provide a "place" for people to meet, free from temporal and spatial constraints (Lysloff 2005), while also providing a sense or spirit of community that holds symbolic meaning for the participants.

Anthropologists Counts and Counts (1996) define community not only as a shared, fixed territory, such as a neighbourhood or small town, but also as relationships and activities based on familiarity and inter-dependence—a social rather than a physical space. This definition fits well with the sense of community based on shared interests and experiences created in cyberspace. Like RVers who form communities when they "camp" at night, virtual communities create an aura of "we-ness" in cyberspace. These communities are neither utopian nor dystopian; they are simply a new manifestation of community. Indeed, Howard et al. (2002: 47) calls the Internet a popular "third place of the twenty-first century" (See Part IV: Gatherings for a discussion of third places). In essence, the Internet is an instant form of social organization; it is not just a place for escape but a place for daily social interaction. Essentially, computer-mediated communication (CMC) has led to the encroachment of virtual space (cyberspace) into physical space (Ward 1999). As such, the concept of community as a physical place is becoming less and less relevant (Correll 1995).

Like physical communities, virtual communities develop personalities, folklore, and acceptable behaviour guidelines ("netiquette"). The language that members of a virtual community use and the identities they form are based on common interests, rather than gender, ethnicity, and class. Yet Rheingold (1993) cautions that these virtual communities are not homogeneous; they are diverse subcultures, each designed to meet the needs and interests of a certain segment of the user population, be it a poetry or theatre club; a site for cooking classes, pet owners, or Trekkies; quilting or organic farming networks; or online fantasy games like MicroMUSE.

54   Arguably, the first icon of computer popular culture was the video game, which created a new subcultural community known as gamers. Like the Internet, which is also audience-controlled to a certain extent, video games and the events that take place during them are controlled by the gamer within the parameters of the game. This is a different experience from reading a book or watching a television program that is producer-controlled.

Video games come in many genres, including action-adventure, puzzles, and strategy and role-playing games. One significant type is the multiplayer online game (MOG). MOGs are two- or three-dimensional video games that allow gamers to create digital characters, called "avatars," who interact with the software and with other players' avatars. These games evolved out of board games, such as *Dungeons & Dragons* (1973) (Steinkuehler & Williams 2006). This form of online gaming is extremely popular, with four million players worldwide, and growing (Meek 2004). Although Oldenburg (1999) does not agree, MOGs are a new form of "third place," which offer disaffected youth, often isolated in suburbia and overscheduled with activities (ballet, piano, soccer), opportunitiesto mask their loneliness. They are a place where people "meet," converse, argue about local politics or sports, and try to make some sense of the world (Boyd 2004). Indeed, online gaming fits the definition of third places better than most physical gathering places, especially when considering the anonymity of gender, ethnicity, age, and class. As with other types of virtual communities, gamer communities develop their own codes of conduct, languages, and taboos.

T. Kanayama's (2000) ethnographic study of virtual communities among Japanese seniors yields some valuable insights into online socialization, as well as the efficacy of online ethnography. Kanayama had already been a participant in the community for two years, serving as a technical volunteer supporter, before beginning her ethnographic research. As a result, members of the virtual community already knew her, and her presence online did not disturb them, thereby avoiding one of the major questions concerning online ethnography: if members of a chat room know a researcher is in the chat room, will their conversations become less typical? On the other hand, if the researcher remains an anonymous or passive participant, then issues of privacy and ethics may be raised. Kanayama solved this quandary by becoming an online participant before becoming an online ethnographer.

Kanayama sought to understand the experiences of elderly people online—how they interacted with others online, and how they constructed online social relationships. She found that elderly Japanese belonging to *senior-ml* enjoyed a strong support network, especially for members experiencing health problems, the death of a spouse, or financial concerns. Interestingly, these seniors did not mask their identities; they used their first names or nicknames online, which in itself is unusual since most Japanese only use first names with close friends and family. Some of the members also felt that the Internet blurred personal characteristics that can create social inequality, in this case, that they were elderly or infirm.

The opportunity for social interaction appeared most important to the people in this study, who might otherwise have been unable to physically enter into social activities outside their homes. They mainly used e-mail for entertainment, socializing, and making plans. Their time on the Internet did not appear to take away from other activities; they merely substituted it for other media, such as television. They also found ways around the limitations of text-based communication (that is, the lack of non-verbal cues) by using various forms of language, such as "emoticons," (graphic depictions of emotions made by keyboard characters; the most common might be the smiley face) archaic Japanese (a strategy similar to youths using slang), regional dialects, and haiku poems to communicate their feelings, thereby blending popular culture (emoticons) with traditional culture (haiku) to make their conversations more interesting and meaningful.

In the same way that Kanayama investigated the virtual community created by these Japanese seniors, Shelley Correll (1995) undertook an ethnographic study of an electronic lesbian café (LC) created through a computer bulletin board system (BBS). In a three-month period in the early 1990s, she became immersed in the daily activities of LC members. She posted a public note on the LC, describing her study and asking for volunteers to be interviewed. Each week she added a new note describing what she had observed and at times would ask members to explain various actions or conversations she had witnessed. Some patrons were interviewed in private and in groups via e-mail, telephone, and in person.

During this era of online communication, bulletin boards did not allow for face-to-face communication, body language, tone, expression of emotions, or verbal speech to add meaning to text-based conversations as is now possible through webcamming, Skype, emoticons, and IM.

Nevertheless, while somewhat dated, Correll's research yields valuable insight into the formation and maintenance of a special interest online community. She asked several important and still relevant questions: how is a virtual community created and sustained given the restrictions of the Internet and computer systems, and what purposes are served by this type of virtual community? How do patrons decide what is real and what is not, and to what extent does online interaction blur the distinctions between reality and fantasy?

Performance theory can be applied to answer these questions. Members of the virtual bar engage in performances that identify them through various personality characteristics. In front stage (or public) performance directed at anyone who visits the site, emotions, appearance, manner, and physical props project personality and identity to an audience who share the values of the community and so enhance group solidarity. "Talk" is ritually regulated to create a sense of shared reality. Patrons are polite in order to create a family-like atmosphere and a sense of reality in the bar. The computer environment allows easy manipulation of their setting but restricts expression of emotions. Members of the bulletin board often move from front stage to less formal and less public backstage performance, which is for members or friends online only and which can mean using private e-mails or coded language that others will not understand. Maintaining closeness, morale, and solidarity through joking, talking informally, and making fun of the audience becomes more important. Even in front stage performances, members use subtle communication that the audience will not understand.

Virtual communities are particularly useful in maintaining anonymity and experimenting with behaviour outside normal experience. They provide a haven or retreat from the outside community's hostility and disapproval. This is particularly evident in forums such as the Lesbian Café where individuals will first make tentative postings as they search for a shared experience and a place to feel at home. Lesbian bars have long provided a welcoming, non-threatening social environment for lesbians to meet people and establish intimate relationships; thus, the formation of a virtual bar in cyberspace was inevitable. A lesbian community, as a virtual community, can create a positive identity, establish intimate relationships, and strengthen group solidarity.

The virtual lesbian bar was patterned after a physical bar, which was verbally constructed by "TJ" on the Lesbian Café website. She described features of her fantasy: a highly polished bar along which drinks can be slid and a pool table, fireplace, and hot tub. Other women "found" this bar and liked its friendly atmosphere. As the café became more established, with more regulars, each woman created her own ritual for "entering" the bar, such as posting a note asking the bartender for a specific drink, thereby announcing her presence. She would also place herself in a specific location in the bar; for example, she might say, "I am going to warm up by the fire" (Correll 1995: 279). This ritual closely resembles that of entering a real bar, thereby creating a common sense of reality, although there are some differences: the café is always open, and women drop by for a cup of coffee, not liquor. This fantasy setting can change when a member mentions a new feature, such as a rocking chair, that becomes a focal point where particular individuals settle themselves. If members stop mentioning a particular spot, it no longer exists. Thus, the verbal description of the bar helps construct a shared sense of reality. Inside the bar, theme parties are common, such as the Super Bowl party when women place wagers online, discuss the plays, complain about referees' calls, and cheer for their team. The LC also keeps members informed about local, national, and international issues important to gays and lesbians; for example, one discussion about gays in the military resulted in socio-political activity to remove barriers against gays in service. Thus, this online community serves most of the functions of a physical community.

The LC offers lesbians without a physical community a place to meet in what Correll calls a surrogate community. Many feel a sense of family and strong social bonds there that they may not enjoy in the real world. As one informant stated, "We are all able to be ourselves here and not worry about fitting in" (Correll 1995: 282). The café also provides a place to be around other lesbians: "Because of the pressures from family and friends, I lead a very straight life. The LC is the only place I can really feel 'at home'" (Correll 1995: 283). It is also a safe outlet, providing anonymity as well as a place for recreation and meeting people: "The bar may be a fantasy, but the friends we make are as real as anywhere" (Correll 1995: 283–84). Friends are made, and these friendships may move outside the virtual into the actual community, which creates a blurring of fantasy and reality.

Online communication both liberates and limits participants. The lack of physical presence takes away the pressure of physical attractiveness and enables people to get to know one another based on personality. This is particularly useful for shy people. Since these online relationships are easier to control because of front stage performance, emotions and responses can be more carefully thought out. For members of these early bulletin boards, communicating emotions was difficult, although they did find some strategies, such as abbreviations (e.g., "lol" for "laugh out loud," still used in IM) and using fonts—typing in all caps to indicate anger. Intimate relationships were also difficult to establish online; face-to-face meeting must eventually occur for the relationship to succeed. Finally, censorship of sexually explicit comments still limits conversations, although members can leave the bar and communicate via e-mail, or, as often happens, sexually graphic discussions are camouflaged in metaphors to slip by the censors.

Correll identified four types of LC participants: regulars, newbies, lurkers, and bashers. Most participants are regulars who are experienced conversationalists on the site and well aware of the norms of behaviour, such as posting notes to specific people. They know the personalities of other regulars and personalize their conversations. They use trademarks in their postings; for example, one member always starts the day at the café by making a pot of gourmet coffee, which other regulars expect her to do. Newbies begin as awkward conversationalists, making rude blunders and apologizing constantly for not knowing the protocol. They are unaware of how to use graphics, tails, upper case letters, and abbreviations to convey emotions. They are greeted with suspicion by regulars, and their legitimacy is questioned, often via e-mail to other regulars. Regulars rebuff newbies with negative sanctions, such as ignoring their posts. Gradually, newbies learn the code of behaviour and begin mimicking the behaviour of regulars, such as ordering drinks, and move into the confidence-gaining stage where they develop their own trademarks and personality traits. Lurkers post very little, preferring to watch and learn. Unlike newbies, lurkers do not make as many blunders when they finally enter the café, having used their time to learn the behaviour codes. Lurkers who are deferent and polite are greeted with warmth and welcome, and they quickly move into the confidence-gaining stage. Bashers are usually male, and their purpose is to harass the lesbian members with hostile comments. Their posts are as awkward as the newbies, which is one of the reasons why newbies are initially greeted with suspicion. Regulars and newbies both launch verbal assaults on, or "flame," bashers, thus escalating the conflict. Eventually, the regulars ignore the bashers, who then go away. Bashers do serve an important social function though: they unite the lesbian community against a common enemy and strengthen the community bonds.

Conclusions

In 1993, Rheingold predicted that the Internet would "become the next great escape medium, in the tradition of radio series, Saturday matinees, soap operas—which means that the new medium will be in some way a conduit for and reflector of our cultural codes, our social subconscious, our images of who 'we might be'" (1993: 8). His predictions have more than come true. Indeed, the Internet complements and supplements other forms of communication, such as phone calls and face-to-face meetings, and has become an integral part of our daily lives, bringing people from diverse cultures and communities into virtual contact. To borrow a metaphor from Laura Miller (1995), the Internet has become a rich soup of world cultures.

Anecdotal information suggests that Internet users readily share their popular culture as well as absorb that of others. Indeed, Mediascape coins the phrase "global cultural flows" (Appadurai 1990) of information, communication, and social behaviour, which, for all intents, eliminates geographical and political boundaries. The Internet appears to be a new manifestation of social community—its virtual communities are not bound to the spatial or even temporal constraints of face-to-face communication. The value of these virtual communities as a social experience **59** and shared reality becomes evident when looking at successful communities such as the Lesbian Café and *senior-ml*.

The question was raised earlier in this chapter of whether the Internet is popular culture. Although scholarly research on this question is limited, the fact that it has so profoundly permeated every aspect of our lives, affecting our social relationships and behaviours, and opening up the world to our fingertips, suggests that the Internet is not only a form of popular culture but also a medium for maintaining, expanding, and sharing popular culture. In Chapter 1, we discussed the political power of popular culture in that it can shape and reflect our ideas, generate cultural resistance and activism, mirror changing social values and practices, and influence the way we understand the world around us. The Internet, perhaps more than any other form of popular culture, does just that.

PART III

ARTISTIC EXPRESSION AND POPULAR CULTURE

Artistic expression, in myriad forms, has sustained people for millennia and often provided them with their cultural identity as well as a sense of stability when so many other changes have been beyond their control. Although there are many expressions of art, for the purpose of this discussion artistic expression refers to folk arts and crafts, body art and adornment, and street art—all of which constitute the art of everyday life.

In keeping with a central theme of *Pop Culture,* the question must be asked: are folk art and body art also performance art? According to Jon Erickson, if theatricalized, then art of whatever kind is also performance, since performance is a way of connecting art with everyday life and eliminating distinctions between high art and popular culture (Erickson 1999).

Although most introductory anthropology texts offer a chapter on artistic expression, during a recent perusal of three current "readers" in anthropology, I failed to find a single article on folk art, body adornment, or indeed any form of aesthetic expression of popular culture. This means either that few anthropologists are studying artistic expression or, more likely, that editors of annual editions do not consider these research endeavours worthy of inclusion. This neglect of the anthropological study of popular artistic expression reflects the wider public's perception of artistic expression as superfluous and impractical.

The study of folk art affords insights into people's everyday lives, their values, and their world view, and despite its apparent invisibility in anthropology, some anthropologists do study folk art. They examine how artists express social structure through their art, its meaning, and the way it illuminates changes in culture. Brian Moeran's (1997) study of the *mingei* folk craft movement in Japan using *ontayaki* pottery is a good example of recent ethnographic research on folk art. This simple craft became a symbol for the *mingei* (people's craft) movement. Moeran demonstrates how collectors, dealers, *mingei* "experts," and consumers (audience) have affected the traditional potters (performers) who, for 250 years, have made objects such as pickle jars, hibachi, storage jars, water crocks, teapots, and dishes, all for everyday use. The word "traditional" refers to art that has a long history of production and, within this historical context, continues to be highly valued by its producers and audience. Over time, and despite their anonymity and seeming freedom to practice their craft, *mingei* crafters have been affected by outside forces. For example, people now request signed pieces, a practice that contradicts the anonymity of folk art and may even threaten community solidarity by favouring one potter over another. The potters have also had to deal with increasing requests for decorative rather than utilitarian pieces, which is a defining feature of their folk art. Thus, this study looked beyond the art itself and into the internal and external forces that influence and shape it.

Street art, otherwise known as graffiti, is a controversial form of popular cultural production with multiple audiences creating multiple interpretations and meanings. Critics, however, refuse to acknowledge that it is a form of folk art. Yet, the study of graffiti can offer some important insights into political discourse and cultural resistance. One area where anthropology can contribute is through the scholarly understanding of culture and cultural context. For example, ethnographer and photographer Susan A. Phillips investigated the cultural life of gangs in Los Angeles from an emic perspective; that is, she considered what the artists themselves thought about the meaning of their art. She compared the graffiti written by Chicano and African-American gangs and hip hop taggers and piecers and demonstrated that graffiti artists encode their graffiti to resonate within their own gangs and cultural context, although this form of communication is shared and understood within a much wider region. She also explored the hybridization of hip hop graffiti as it flowed from the east to the west coast. Phillips's insights offer an added dimension to the understanding of graffiti as a cultural device used by marginalized youth to communicate with multiple audiences.

The anthropology of body has become a significant focus of study in the discipline. Body art and adornment express individual and cultural identity, in essence sending out messages: "I belong to this club, faction, socio-economic class ..." or "I am making myself more attractive because...." Anthropologists have always described the physical nature of people in their study group; for example, anthropologist Lars Krutak (1997) has conducted a comparative analysis of tattooing practices among the Inuit of Alaska, Canada, and Greenland, and the St. Lawrence Yupiget, and tattooed mummies from Europe and Asia. However, the study of body art and adornment in Western societies has lagged behind until recently. Despite this seeming neglect, anthropologist Neil Whitehead believes that anthropologists are interested in body modification and its many messages in contemporary North American society where body art is also a medium for resistance and power (quoted in Tanenbaum 2004).

In the following chapters, the significance of artistic expression will be further articulated as we examine the ways in which people recreate and beautify themselves and their surroundings and their reasons for doing so. Chapter 6 presents a cross-cultural examination of the everyday folk art of people around the world, its symbolism and cultural value, and the way that artistic expression is embedded in socio-economic, political, and religious realities. We will consider the power of street art and Palestinian graffiti in political commentary and resistance to perceived hegemonies and even foreign occupation. Chapter 7 continues this line of investigation as we explore how body art and adornment, especially prison tattooing, creates a sense of identity, community, and resistance.

What do Oaxaca woodcarvings, patchwork quilts, Ukrainian Easter eggs, street murals, and giant milk bottles have in common? They are all examples of popular culture known as folk art. Folk art is described as utilitarian pieces, such as pottery vessels, that have been decorated or beautified in some way. Yet, these pieces of art are more than useful or attractive objects; folk art also explores the non-material components of human existence and often symbolizes a community and its social and cultural heritage. It provides opportunities for individual expression and the creation of kinship between artists. Folk art is also a forum for social and political commentary. In the 1960s, Jesse Telfair created the Freedom Quilt when she lost her job for attempting to register to vote in Georgia (Fordham 2007). This quilt became not only a symbol of Telfair's strength in the face of adversity but also a larger commentary on the African-American community's struggles for equality and freedom in the United States. Indeed, "pop" art has become an integral part of many resistance movements as pop artists engage in political commentary on war, race, and gender (Clark 1993).

The term "popular art" is often used synonymously with folk art, although it may encompass art forms not readily identified with everyday life. "Fine art" is also a term often used to distinguish between forms of art. Fine art is artwork that has considerable monetary value and prestige attached to it, has been created by formally trained and recognized artists, and is difficult to obtain (e.g., a Renoir painting), while folk art is created by informally trained local artists, is readily available, and is not that highly valued beyond the local community, although interest in some local folk art is increasing to the point where it has become commodified cultural production traded on the global market. (for example, Egyptian papyrus paintings). The artisans of folk art are usually anonymous; artistic individuality and fame are not nearly as important as the continued perpetuation of traditional styles, symbols, and designs (Sozanski 2007).

Folk art is remarkably diverse, creating some challenges when determining just what is or is not folk art. It can take any number of forms: toys (Russian nesting dolls), pottery (African-American face vessels), paintings (Huichol yarn paintings from Mexico), textiles (Hmong textiles from Laos and *molas* stitchery from the San Blas Islands), woodwork (Puerto Rican festival masks), decorations (*wycinanki* paper cuts from Poland), and so on. Although considered art work of the common people, some folk art is quite rare and precious, such as a mandolin-type stringed instrument from Latin America made from an armadillo shell decorated with etched mother-of-pearl inlay (Sozanski 2007).

In this chapter we will focus on the meaning of folk art to both the artist-performers and the audience. We will begin with a brief cross-cultural examination of local folk art. Folk art is inextricably linked to other aspects of culture, such as religion. Indeed, religious symbolism is an important element of folk art, as you will see in the discussion of Ukrainian Easter eggs. Most folk art also has a functional or utilitarian purpose; for example, a Navajo sand painting is used in healing and blessing ceremonies. We will consider the role of quilting in popular culture, beyond the primary purpose of coverings for warmth to expressions of cultural identity and a voice for socio-political commentary. The social and political complexities inherent in street art and graffiti will become apparent in our discussion of graffiti in Toronto, Rio de Janeiro, and the occupied West Bank in Israel.

64

What is Folk Art?

Folk art makes a statement regarding what matters to the artist and the audience and what kind of world these players inhabit. Indeed, folk art is often representative of our cultural identity and cultural heritage. Between 1810 and 1865, many African-American slaves worked as artisans at Edgefield Potteries in South Carolina (Gianis 2006). In their spare time these artisans made their own pottery, creating alkaline-glazed stoneware jugs shaped like human faces and so known as face vessels. Although the identity of the artisans and the purpose of the face vessels are lost in time, they may have had religious or burial significance since they have been found on Underground Railroad routes and in gravesites. Regardless of their original purpose, today they are symbolic of the African-American slave culture. So, too, the origin of *wycinanki* paper cuts in Poland is also unknown. Some accounts suggest this folk art originated when farm houses did not have glass windows. Farmers hung sheep skins over the openings, then, in order to get more light, they cut out small openings that soon became decorative as well as functional. Other accounts suggest making the cut-outs was a form of relaxation in rural areas. Today *wycinanki* is given to family members as gifts or sold to tourists (Polish Art Center n.d.). Both of these forms of folk art are expressions of everyday life.

The Easter custom of dyeing eggs originated in Egypt for the pharaonic rite of spring known as *Shamm al Nisim*, "sniffing the breezes" (Kup 1956). Decorating eggs has been a rite of fertility and a symbol of rebirth in both ancient and contemporary cultures. Crimson eggs honouring the blood of Christ are exchanged in Greece, while green eggs are exchanged in Germany and Austria on Maundy Thursday (Holy Thursday, the Thursday before Easter). Some Slavic peoples decorate their eggs in gold and silver patterns, while Armenians decorate hollow eggs with pictures of the Virgin Mary, Christ, or other religious symbols (Sadler 2004). Giving decorated eggs (both real and candy) to children has become a time-honoured tradition in many countries today. Obviously, the decorating and exchanging of eggs at Easter is a form of popular culture as well as an important religious ritual that has survived to modern times.

Decorating eggs at Easter is also an ethnic tradition. This is particularly evident in the Ukraine where an intricate art form called *pysanky* has been handed down for generations. Annie Fedorak, a Ukrainian craftswoman, explained to me how the eggs are made. First, elaborate patterns are drawn on the shell using a stylus dipped in hot wax—the wax protects the egg from the dye—then the egg is dyed a light colour, like yellow. The artist again decorates the egg with hot wax, sealing in the yellow paint. The process continues, adding more wax designs and colours, essentially decorating in reverse order. The symbols and designs used on *pysanky* eggs have many meanings (Tostanoski n.d.): wheat asks for a bountiful harvest; animals, in particular deer, symbolize prosperity; dots depict stars or the Virgin's tears; a fish is a sign of Christ; and any form of the cross signifies the Resurrection of Christ, death, and suffering. In pre-Christian times, an eight-pointed star symbolized the sun god; later the star represented Christ. Designs that circle the entire egg symbolize eternity. Colours are also symbolic: red represents the sun, life, and joy; yellow, wealth and fertility; and green, spring and plants. Ukrainian artisans brought *pysanky* folk art to other countries when they emigrated, and, unlike many other traditions, the skill is still passed on to the next generation.

The mythology of a culture is often represented in its folk art. Yarn paintings of the Huichol people living in the Sierra Madre Mountains in Mexico embody their history and mythology. Shamans create yarn paintings while in an altered state of consciousness brought on by imbibing peyote cactus. Strands of brightly coloured yarn are applied to boards thinly coated with beeswax. The animals, colours, and symbols created in yarn are representative of their belief system and explain their world view: blue is south and feminine, while red is east and masculine (McGee 1998).

Russian nesting dolls (*matryoshka*) are a popular form of folk art, partly because the oldest dolls represent Russian myths, legends, and fairy tales, and partly because some recent ones are caricatures of Russian politicians, such as the "Gorbi" doll. Indeed, dolls representing Russian politicians are a form of relatively benign cultural resistance. These anthropomorphized "take apart" dolls are a modern manifestation of a Russian folk tradition borrowed from the Byzantines. One pulls apart the largest wooden, exquisitely painted doll to find a similarly painted, smaller doll inside; pull apart that one and a still smaller doll is revealed and so on down to the very smallest. Most traditional nesting dolls portray a sturdy peasant woman dressed in traditional clothing and a head scarf; she is a symbol of fertility and motherhood. To many people, the nesting dolls are "both sculpture and painting, image and soul of Russia" (RussianLegacy.com 2003).

The meanings people attach to their popular culture can come to symbolize more than their original purpose. Quilt-making, an age-old craft found in many cultures, has been transformed into a symbol of hope in the West. The AIDS Memorial Quilt was created in 1987 in remembrance of those who have died from AIDS, to create awareness in the audience, and to present a message of hope to both the producers and the audience that this disease will be eradicated (The AIDS Memorial Quilt n.d.). Cleve Jones started the AIDS Memorial Quilt in San Francisco with a single panel and the name of a friend who had died of the disease. Now containing 6,000 panels, with the names of 91,000 victims, the quilt has become "the largest piece of community folk art in the world" (McKinley 2007: A16) and the most recognizable symbol of the AIDS crisis. The AIDS Memorial Quilt is thus a prime example of political commentary through folk art.

The earliest evidence of quilting is found on a 5,400-year-old Egyptian tomb carving that resembles a quilted garment (Hoffman 2001), and the Leningrad Institute of Archaeology houses a quilted floor covering from the first century BC. Quilting arrived in North America in the early 1700s with Amish settlers from Germany and Switzerland (World Wide Quilting Page 2006). Like other forms of popular culture, quilts are a mirror of the economic, social, and political environment of the time. In North America, patchwork and striped quilts were constructed of scraps of material or even feed sacks in the 1930s when fabric was in short supply. During the settlement of the American West, friends and relatives sent pieces of their clothing along as remembrances; these scraps were later made into charm quilts. Charm quilt folklore suggests that if a repeated fabric is used, it brings good luck. These same pioneers held quilting bees that offered women in isolated American and Canadian farming communities an occasion for socializing and to show off their skills. The women worked together to create a quilt, and when it was finished their families would join them for a feast that gave the host of the quilting bee a chance to show off her culinary skills and gain status in the community. Quilting can also play a role in preserving history. The Hmong of Laos have made quilts (*pa ndaa*) for thousands of years. These quilts have become both a freedom banner and a documentation of their history (Lee n.d.).

Graffiti Street Art

"A wall without pictures is broken" (Anonymous graffiti artist, *Eye on Brazil*, America Plus, 1 December 2006).

The question has often been asked: is graffiti art? Many consider graffiti writing criminal vandalism, but to others, especially the graffiti artists themselves, street art is a way of expressing ideas and thoughts and bringing colour to a dreary world. Researchers have asked some important questions concerning graffiti: who writes it? For what reason(s)? Who is/are the audience(s)? Answers to these questions may shed light on whether a particular form of graffiti deserves the label of art.

Some of the criticism against graffiti is suspect. Susan Phillips (1999) believes that some audiences see graffiti as a visible reminder of urban decay, delinquency, and degeneracy in youth and so criticize it to justify their fears and prejudice. Some criticism may even be a veil for racial intolerance. Yet, defining graffiti as either art or vandalism is overly simplistic—graffiti art is acceptable in some circumstances (in art galleries), but in others it is not (subway tagging) (Bowen 1999). The term "graffiti" is also problematic in that it is an important designation for the artists and one they want to promote as a serious art form, regardless of any negativity attached to the term.

Graffiti's value as a vehicle of expression has been typically underestimated. According to Ley and Cybriwsky (1974: 491), wall graffiti can be an indicator of "attitudes, behavioural dispositions, and social processes in settings where direct measurement is difficult." Austin (2002: 450) suggests that graffiti is "one of the major vernacular aesthetic movements of this past century," and Baca (1995: 136) points out that graffiti art "was the first visual art form entirely developed by youth culture." This way of thinking appears to be slowly taking hold: on December 1, 2006, *Eye on Brazil* featured graffiti as an artistic mode for expressing ideas, and since the 1970s graffiti art has been shown in New York art galleries (Bowen 1999). This change in attitude reflects a growing acceptance that at least some forms of graffiti are part of contemporary art culture.

Often called guerrilla art—unauthorized art in public spaces (Hathaway 2007)—graffiti has, in many cases, evolved from gang-related activities. Indeed, graffiti art crosses boundaries between street culture, youth subcultures, and artistic communities (Bowen 1999). Graffiti also provides a medium for cultural resistance. Juan Llamosas of the Argentine studio *La Vertical*, believes graffiti in South America has been infused with grunge and punk ideas, all forms of resistance to state hegemony (Digit 2006).

On the streets of Rio de Janeiro, paint sprays of scrawling names and epithets have been replaced with eye-catching displays of artistic wonder. This graffiti resembles the art work of Warhol, Kandinsky, da Vinci, and Peter Blake, but it also bears a resemblance to Japanese *anime* that has been mixed with original work representing the graffiti artist's life experiences. According to Todd Baxter (2006), graffiti artists do not want to destroy the walls they paint on, they simply want to paint. Rio graffiti reflects the stark realities of life in a city where economically depressed citizens co-exist alongside the wealthy. In the words of Acme, an acclaimed Rio graffiti artist: "I go out to paint without any fixed idea...I get the inspiration as soon as I get there. I think about my friends, some who are living in *favelas* (shantytowns) and who are sleeping all day, who are not participating in society. Their paradise of Rio is lost quickly. We have got to get them to think, to reawaken them" (Baxter 2006: 2). To do this, graffiti artists are working to brighten up the shantytowns, using colours on the walls to bring hope and strength to members of the community. "I have to do what I have to do," Acme explains. "I can't leave these walls all blank and abandoned here, nobody else fixes it so it's left to us to take care of business" (Baxter 2006: 2).

Marginalized and disaffected Puerto Rican youth began to create hip hop graffiti in New York subways in the 1960s and 1970s. Since then, biased media reports have linked graffiti writing to crime and vandalism because street gangs use graffiti tags—signatures or marks—as boundary markers for their territories and to make public claim to a neighbourhood (Bowen 1999). Graffiti became a means for disenfranchised and impoverished youth in the hip hop subculture to feel empowered and to express their resistance to the establishment. Subways, as a meeting place for many cultural worlds, from the suburbs to the inner city, were a perfect medium for their messages, and this is where graffiti found a home.

In the Greater Toronto area, graffiti art enjoyed a resurgence in popularity in the 1990s (Bowen 1999). Graffiti began in Toronto as tagging, but soon evolved into colourful murals covering entire walls. Graffiti artists gradually grew more interested in the quality of their work, and they employed formal elements of composition, colour, and design. This change in attitude separated them from their counterparts in New York. Also, unlike New York graffiti writers, most Toronto graffiti artists secure permission from property owners before painting, and their art contains little that is subversive or even political. On the other hand, Toronto artists are adamant about their right to self-expression, and use this right as a rationale for breaking the law if necessary (Bowen 1999).

Anthropologist Tracy Bowen set out to redefine graffiti through the narratives of Toronto graffiti artists. She asked some important questions: why have artists chosen graffiti as a means of public self-expression? How do they relate to their audience? Toronto graffiti artists consider their primary audience to be other graffiti artists, who are most able to appreciate their work, while outsiders are a secondary audience. Informants in Bowen's study wanted audiences to find their work "entertaining, thought-provoking, and enjoyable" (Bowen 1999: 33), but unlike most graffiti artists, they feel little need to write political or social messages. Nor do they mark their territory as often as counterparts in other regions. This style of graffiti runs counter to the highly politicized graffiti in Palestine.

Ley and Cybriwsky (1974: 492) call graffiti "the twilight zone of communication." This has certainly proved true in political struggles, such as that between the Palestinians and Israelis. Palestinians have been denied cultural and political expression in a public forum; therefore, writing on the walls is a way to respond to Israeli military rule. Graffiti tags began cropping up in the occupied West Bank during the late 1980s as much more than artistic expression or even an identity marker—they were a medium for expressing political resistance against an occupying force. Graffiti circumvents censorship and gives voice to this resistance—at least for a short time—and is a relatively benign form of civil disobedience. The actual production of graffiti occurs within the context of censorship, breaking rules, and creating public space, and it is part of a larger resistance requiring non-payment of taxes, boycott of Israeli goods, and raising the Palestinian flag. This form of graffiti lacks the finesse of New York tagging or the artistic talent of Toronto and Rio artists; the hastily drawn messages left by Palestinian youth are more important than the style, as is the tag or signature identifying the political faction responsible for the writing. Thus, Palestinian youth have taken the territoriality of New York street gang graffiti to a new level.

Graffiti in Palestine became the "silent narratives accompanying acts of resistance" (Peteet 1996: 143). It signals the continuance of the resistance to Israeli occupation in Palestine and is a way of announcing the latest moves of various resistance factions: "Today's graffiti are tomorrow's headlines" (Ley & Cybriwsky 1974). According to one young Palestinian woman: "It's kind of like reading the newspaper. As I walk to the main road, I scan the walls quickly to see what is newly written. I already know the old graffiti and usually they are blocked out after a few days anyway. I try to quickly read the new graffiti. I think of it as a way of getting the news. Often I laugh because some of them are funny" (Peteet 1996: 151). Most Palestinians follow the graffiti closely when things are happening; it becomes "a reading of the streets" (Peteet 1996: 151).

In the 1990s, anthropologist Julie Peteet (1996) lived in Beit Hanina, a small suburb of Jerusalem. Here she conducted an extensive study of "writing on the walls," an activity that was particularly apparent in this area, and learned to "read" graffiti from other Palestinians. She explored graffiti as a form of cultural production used for resistance, asking how and under what circumstances it is produced and what its production means to the writers (performers) and audiences. She found that graffiti has multiple audiences—from Israeli and Palestinian citizens going about their daily business, to graffiti writers from competing factions, to the Israeli soldiers charged with destroying the messages. All of these audiences "read" and interpret the messages in different ways.

For Palestinians, graffiti are cultural artefacts used to challenge and transform power relations. Graffiti validates both community and resistance, generates public discourse on cultural traditions (such as the wearing of the veil), records history and events, commemorates martyrs, and supplies directives to the audiences—for example, "No taxes without representation." In other words, the Palestinian community thinks "out loud" through graffiti (Peteet 1996: 141–42). To the Israelis, graffiti is a dangerous symbol of the political problems and the failure of the Israeli government and military to quell the Palestinian uprising. Israelis considered "any live performance in front of an audience to be dangerous thanks to theatre's acknowledged capacity to incite audiences" (Slyomovics 1991: 27, quoted in Peteet 1996: 141).

Writing graffiti is often used as a rite of passage into adulthood and the resistance movement—a new recruit shows his or her commitment to the resistance by writing graffiti (Peteet 1996). The dangerous act creates a collective identity, and a sense of community is created among graffiti writers through their common political experience and social defiance. Palestinian graffiti acknowledges this community and is both self-reflective and self-critical (Peteet 1996). Graffiti, then, links diverse Palestinians under a common goal: to remove the occupiers through civil disobedience.

Graffiti walls have become a symbol of the political struggle in the West Bank—Palestinian youth write their messages at night, Israeli soldiers efface the messages with paint early in the morning, the youths rewrite their messages the next night, and the battle for the walls continues. This battle has become a contest over place; since Palestinians are denied expression in public spaces, graffiti transforms these places into an arena for communication. To the Palestinian youth, graffiti is a way to challenge Israeli occupation and a symbol of their refusal to acquiesce or accept current conditions. To the Israelis, graffiti is a sign of defiance and lawlessness. The stone walls used for graffiti, and the messages themselves, become "weapons of communication, assault, and defense" (Peteet

1996: 139). Like Afro-Cuban rap music, graffiti has become an avenue for resistance, a popular cultural production used for political and social commentary aimed at a multitude of audiences.

Conclusions

Folk art is one of the more visible forms of popular culture. Unlike music, television, or film, folk art is created *by* ordinary people, not just *for* ordinary people, and it is where popular culture begins. Folk art is a mirror of cultural traditions, but it also challenges prevailing world views and may become a vehicle for resistance. Despite the modernization and globalization processes that threaten so many other traditions, folk art continues to flourish and in some cases, as we saw with quilting, is becoming increasingly popular.

Ukrainian Easter egg decorating is steeped in religious symbolism, which in part explains its enduring quality and the ease with which this ethnic tradition has diffused to North America with immigrants. Yet, it remains limited to a few artisans within a limited number of ethnic groups. Quilting, on the other hand, is a world-wide phenomenon and as such has many meanings: the joy of creating a work of beauty; the sense of community and cultural identity created as quilters work together, sharing experiences and a common cause; and the socio-political messages offered in some quilts. All of these meanings are important and symbolize the powerful impact of quilting on both the producers and audience.

The question was posed: is graffiti art? A better question would be: when does graffiti become art? Graffiti writing—slogans, protests, and territorial markers—are a form of print warfare, while the colourful wall murals that have evolved out of slogan graffiti are closer to what most people would consider art. Nevertheless, both styles of graffiti contain messages, offer social and political commentary, and hold meaning for the artists and their audiences. Peteet (1996: 144) calls writing graffiti a "performative element in a rite of passage into the resistance." It is the voice of those who feel voiceless.

Despite the "ordinariness" of the folk art discussed here, out of thousands of flourishing styles and designs found around the world, the folk art of everyday people in their everyday lives has a much greater impact on culture than the finest painting or sculpture in that it holds myriad messages that are interpreted, contested, and even transformed by its audiences.

As far as we know, humans have always found ways to adorn and modify their bodies, whether through temporary make-up and clothing styles or more permanent piercings, painting, and tattooing. Why do people endure all sorts of pain and discomfort, even bodily danger, in order to enhance their physical appearance? Despite the incredible variation in body art, the reasons and meanings attached to this practice appear to be culturally based: to convey personal identity and individuality; mark important stages in life; record historic events; indicate group member-ship and solidarity; announce status, position, and wealth; appease the spirits or embody religious beliefs; proclaim resistance against hegemonic powers; and, of course, enhance beauty and attractiveness. For those in the West, where body art is becoming increasingly popular, the reasons are no less complex: resisting the status quo, symbolizing identity, paying tribute to significant events and people, and enhancing attractiveness.

Body art is not, nor has it ever been, a frivolous activity; rather, it is embedded in cultural symbolism, values, beliefs, and world view. In some cultures, body art follows a prescribed pattern, limiting choices to acceptable cultural norms, while in others it is constantly changing as individuals choose from a wide range of styles and designs, each of which bestow identity, status, and acceptance within a particular group. The interconnectedness of many cultural practices is also evident in body art. Oftentimes, as seen among the people of central Borneo, tattoos have religious significance—in this case shielding people from dangerous spir-its (Schildkrout 2001). Men in Tierra del Fuego painted their bodies in a ritual to transform themselves into spirits for initiation rites. Tattoos as a form of body art, then, have been used to transcend gender, class, and ethnic and national identity (Schildkrout 2001).

Throughout *Pop Culture*, we have addressed the concept of perfor-mance. The question of what constitutes performance becomes even more uncertain when considering body art. According to Jon Erickson (1999), body art is performance art when its presentation becomes theatricalized, and Jones (1998) suggests that it is performance between the spectacle and the spectator. In this discussion we will cast a wide net, beginning with an exploration of body painting and piercing in several diverse cultures.

We will consider the many meanings of body art and ask the questions: why do people alter their bodies? And how do we interpret character, status, and image through body art? According to anthropologist Margo Demello (1993), the human body can become a landscape for symbolically marking gender, ethnicity, and class. Using her ethnographic research, we will examine prison tattooing and its political power in resisting prison hegemony and creating a sense of identity and community.

About Body Art

Body painting is a common form of self-expression in many indigenous cultures. Nuba men of Sudan paint their bodies white on one side and black on the other. In New Guinea, the women paint their faces red, blue, and white, while young Trobrianders use black and white vegetable dyes to paint designs on their faces and rub charmed coconut oil into their skin to make it shine in an attempt to appear more attractive to the opposite sex. In the West, body painting is not that common, although New York's East Village punks paint their bodies in multicolours, and European Goths paint their bodies white and their lips and eyes black. For some, body paint is a way to communicate ancient mythology, values, and beliefs; it is also a way to create a visually distinct group (Polhemus & Randall 2000). Body paint can also signify major events or stages in a person's life. For example, in Nuba, only male elders or members of older age grades can wear deep yellow or black paint.

Gender also plays a role in body painting; Nuba men decorate their bodies elaborately, while women wear simple decoration appropriate to their kinship group. Among the nomadic Wodaabes people (also known as the Bororo) in northern Niger, young men dress in extravagant costumes complete with embroidered vests, head bands, and necklaces. For the *gerewol* courting ritual, where the men essentially put on a beauty pageant, they wear dramatic make-up—clay masks to lighten their skin, a long white line painted from hairline to nose tip, eyes lined with dark kohl, and lips darkened. Once ready, the men form a *fijol* line, humming and clapping their hands, and slowly form a circle while chanting and swaying. The exhaustive dancing can go on at length, and eventually the most handsome men are chosen by young women. This pairing may result in marriage (Jefkin 2004).

Body piercing is the puncturing of the skin with holes for decorative, religious, or symbolic purpose. Piercing the earlobe is an almost universal practice, followed by nose and lip piercings. The Masai of Kenya pierce their ears, then stretch the holes by inserting increasingly larger plugs and wearing heavier jewellery. This is a common body modification practice among indigenous peoples around the world. Among the Kayapo of the

Amazon, leaders enlarge their bottom lip by inserting plates known as labrets or lip plugs. For a Kayapo leader, these plugs are symbols of his status, manhood, and oratory skills (Jefkin 2004).

Among the Unangan (also known as Aleuts) of Alaska, there is a long history of body piercing, in particular of the nose, ears, and lip (Krutak 2006b). This ancient practice embodies spiritual beliefs and hunting practices by honouring animal spirits. Nose pins are the most common piercing; both men and women are pierced shortly after birth and adorned with an eagle feather, sea lion whisker, or bone. Ear ornaments are also very common. The piercings are a visual sign of incorporation into an identifiable group and also fulfill the need for personal expression, social display, celebration, embodied religious beliefs, and a link to nature. In a similar vein, a new mark is given to men of the Bume of Ethiopia during a complex ceremony after a hunt or kill; thus, body piercing reflects their success as hunters and is a record of personal achievement (Jefkin 2004).

By 1993, body piercing had grown in popularity in the West, "blamed" partly on Alicia Silverstone's navel-piercing in Aerosmith's *Cryin'* video (Epstein 2001). Westerners enthusiastically adopted piercings; ear, nostril, septum, lip, eyebrow, navel, nipple, and genital piercings are most common. For many, piercings symbolize taking control of their own bodies: "My body wasn't mine until I claimed it through piercing. I didn't do it for fashion. I make all my own jewellery and use it to create balance within me, that is very important. I like modifying and recreating my body in many ways, this is exciting" (Polhemus & Randall 2000).

Tattoos are an ancient form of body art that has enjoyed several reincarnations. Tattooing is the permanent injection of pigment into the skin, one or two centimetres in depth, to create a design. Currently, it is an extremely popular form of body decoration among Western youth, but archaeological records suggest that tattooing was practiced at least 7,000 years ago among the Scythian cultures of Siberia (Sanders 2001), and Egyptian royalty were tattooing by 4000 BC. Interpretations of Egyptian remains suggest that the geometric designs on the limbs and bodies of royal women may have had medicinal or fertility powers, and tattoos may have served as permanent protective amulets, especially during pregnancy (Lineberry 2007). The corpse of a 5,000-year-old hunter discovered in an Alpine glacier had 15 tattoos, indicating that tattooing was also a common custom in Europe among the Gauls, Goths, Teutons, Picts, Scots, and Britons. Tattooing diffused from the Middle East to India, China, Japan, and the Pacific Island cultures by 4000 BC; the Edo Period (1600–1868) in Japan was the height of Asian tattoo artistry (Polhemus & Randall 2000).

Although indigenous cultures have practiced tattooing since ancient times and continue to do so, the same is not true in Europe. In AD 325,

Constantine banned tattooing in Europe, and this ban remained in effect until Captain James Cook brought the practice back from the South Pacific in 1760. Indeed, Cook was the one who coined the expression "ta-tu." Cook's crew enthusiastically embraced tattoos, and the stereotype of sailors and tattoos was born. In the nineteenth century, tattooing became a popular "fad" among European aristocracy that later spread to the elite in the United States. However, fears of catching diseases led to a decline in its popularity in the early twentieth century. Only the lower classes continued to tattoo, and for this they were considered uncouth and uncivilized. This nefarious reputation is likely what attracted countercultures to the practice, such as the Hippies in the 1960s, and caused a tattoo renaissance among young people looking for ways to visibly express their resistance to the Establishment.

Tattooing in the 1960s became an identity marker, announcing group membership. Hippies used tattoos to communicate their ideologies; the peace symbol, for instance, was a common tattoo. In the 1970s, more women adopted tattooing as a symbol of their gender identity and newfound independence. This was occurring in other countries as well; in Cuba, tattooing was considered subversive and criminal until the 1980s when popular culture dictated that tattoos were "cool" (Krutak 2005). The Cuban government begrudgingly gave its approval to licensed artists, labelling tattooing authentic folk art.

Tattooing, as an art and as a cultural practice, embodies a complex set of meanings. Tattoos are often used to celebrate stages in life or rites of passage, for example, moving through puberty into adulthood. This was the case for the Li people of Hainan Island, China, who historically tattooed their face, hands, and legs in geometric patterns (Krutak 2006a). Tattooing was more common among women, although men tattooed three blue rings around their wrists for medicinal purposes. Motifs and designs varied from one tribal group to another and even from one family to another. During the rite of passage, a young girl was tattooed on her nape, then on her face and throat. Over the next three years, her arms and legs were also tattooed. First her arms were stencilled with Chinese ink, then a thorn was used to prick her skin, followed by rubbing soot mixed with water into the mark. Usually the first tattooing was followed by an elaborate puberty ceremony. To the Li, this tattooing added to the girl's attractiveness, signalled her eligibility for marriage, and provided a way for ancestors to recognize their kin after death. According to a *National Geographic Magazine* writer living among the Li in the 1930s, observers could "read the village, social standing, and identity" in a woman's tattoos (Krutak 2006a). Today, the practice of tattooing has all but disappeared among the Li people; only a few elderly women still display the geometric designs.

The Rashaayda Bedouin of eastern Sudan use tattooing to communicate identity and symbolize their relations with others. Rashiidy women tattoo their bodies in three places: the forearms, the lower half of their face, and their upper legs and thighs (Young 1994). Although the arm tattoos are merely decorative, the face and leg tattoos are private symbols reserved for their loved ones, since the veils they wear cover their entire face, except eyes, concealing facial tattoos, and their long robes hide their legs. Indeed, an unmarried woman may have her thigh tattooed with a man's camel brand to announce her love for him. The purpose of tattooing can also change or be modified; among Polynesians tattoos were mainly used to declare political rank and status, but recently they have also been used to proclaim ethnic identity (Schildkrout 2001).

For Westerners, tattooing has become a popular practice that transcends age, gender, class, and ethnic boundaries (Kosut 2006). It has moved from the fringes of society into mainstream popular culture, and in the last decade of the twentieth century it enjoyed tremendous growth in popularity among people from all walks of life. A 2006 study published in the *Journal of American Academy of Dermatology* found that 24 per cent of adults aged 18 to 50 had a tattoo, and a 2003 Harris poll reported 36 per cent of 25- to 29-year-olds had some form of body art (Breslin 2006). Tattoos often symbolize difference, of belonging to a distinct subculture outside mainstream society. Fantasy and science fiction illustrations, ethnic designs, photorealist portraiture, and abstract art are all common designs. Some of the tattoos are so intricate and of such high quality that they may be considered fine art. Nonetheless, tattooing is still an identity marker and still represents non-conventionalism.

Anthropologist Diane Bell marvels at the change in attitude toward women getting a tattoo from 20 years ago: "For a woman to have done that, it would have marked her out as a 'bad girl.' Somehow or other we've shifted right out of that. Now it's 'my body, my choice'" (Handwerk 2002: 1). Although tattoos are most often linked to youth in Western cultures, Bell sees middle-class suburban women, doctors, and lawyers being attracted to tattoos. She believes that the media has a lot to do with this increasing popularity—cultural icons such as rock stars, athletes, and other celebrities sporting tattoos has elevated their status.

Kosut (2006) suggests that tattooing will eventually lose its popular appeal as more and more mainstream individuals (middle-class suburbanites) acquire them. As the practice becomes embedded in mainstream culture, it will lose its shock value. However, unlike other forms of fashion that disappear as quickly as they appear, tattoos are a permanent body modification, which makes them more culturally significant. While designs hold meaning, the process is also important in that the method used creates a cultural body along with clearly marked social boundaries based on gender, ethnicity, social position, and class. This is particularly true of prison tattoos.

Anthropologist Margo Demello (1993) spent three years conducting field research among the American tattoo community, having gained access as a member herself. She met with ex-convicts at a tattoo shop in Modesta, California, near a California Youth Authority facility, and interviewed male convicts and guards at Folsom State Penitentiary. She concentrated on the manner in which tattoos convey ethnic and social identity, status, and a sense of community within the institutionalized environment of a prison, as well as on the outside.

Tattoo culture in prison is hierarchical and fairly structured. Demello (1993: 10) identified four separate categories of tattooing: professional, semi-professional, street, and prison, based on "social, economic, artistic and technological factors." Professional tattooing most closely resembles popular folk art; at times professional tattooing has even been called fine art. It is professional tattooing that has become increasingly popular among middle-class mainstream populations in Western societies. On the other end of this spectrum, at the bottom of the hierarchy, is prison tattooing.

While tattoo designs are meaningful, Demello discovered that the process of acquiring a tattoo is also important. The type of tattoo and method used to make the tattoo broadcast to the prison population and the outside world the social position of the bearer. In essence, the process of becoming tattooed creates a visible reminder of the convict's individual and group identity, while also pointing out the differences between prisoners and the outside world. For the most part, prison tattoos are fairly primitive, using a method known as hand picking: a sewing needle is wrapped in string and dipped in India ink or the ink from a ballpoint pen. The needle punctures the skin repeatedly to form a line, followed by shading with the string. These tattoos are usually on public parts of the body—for example, the arms or hands—and are easily read by others. This type of self-tattooing is not very highly regarded, partly because of its crude appearance and partly because the production of homemade tattoos signifies the low socio-economic status of the bearer and his inability to access or afford a professional tattoo.

The tattoo hierarchy is also associated with age—youth in the juvenile penal system are most likely to get hand-picked tattoos. By the time they "graduate" to adult prison, they may begin getting better quality machine-made tattoos, often to cover the more primitive ones. This behaviour is also common with Chicanos and bikers who cover their street tattooing (tattoos created outside a tattoo shop) with professional tattoos as soon as they can afford it.

The second method of tattooing in prison uses a homemade rotary machine constructed using a motor from a small appliance, such as a razor or Walkman, connected to a guitar string or sewing needle, which vibrates up and down in the barrel of a Bic pen. The machine is hooked up to a nine-volt AC adaptor. The tattoos created by these machines are more controlled, with finer, smoother lines, and monochromatic (black only) subtle shading. Tattooists who use these machines are known as "scratchers." Despite its simplicity and its association with men from lower social positions, the mainstream tattooing community has appropriated this black-only style, blurring the boundaries between the two communities.

78 Prison tattooing imagery is fairly diverse. The most popular prison tattoo is *loca,* which gives the name of the convict's home neighbourhood or gang affiliation and serves as a reminder of the community the convict left behind. *Loca* may also announce the ethnic identity of the convict, which has important social ramifications when he comes into contact with rival groups. Bars, scales of justice, and other symbols that reflect life experiences are also popular, although a tear tattooed below the outside corner of the eye is the most popular and recognizable icon. Each tear represents a prison term served or the number of people the convict has killed. Demello (1993) calls this a self-inflicted brand.

Tattooing in prison is illegal, and convicts who get a tattoo are taking a considerable risk, although participating in a forbidden activity in itself affects their status. Indeed, the prison population is divided between those who get tattoos and those who do not. According to Demello's estimate, half of the prisoners, mostly Chicanos and whites, have tattoos. One informant told her that Chicanos make the best tattooists. Demello's informants called tattooing the second best hustle (next to drugs) in the prison system. The tattoos are paid for with drugs, food, or cash.

An informal honour code is in place; older tattooists prefer not to tattoo young convicts, especially first timers, since having a tattoo can limit their life chances, such as employment, once they are released. Repeat offenders, however, tend to have their older, cruder tattoos covered over with better tattoos, and empty spaces on their bodies filled in for complete coverage. Convicts released from prison may continue the process, using the same prison method, since they likely cannot afford professional work.

Tattoos are border markers, creating divisions between high and low culture, as we saw above. Prison tattoos express cultural categories of class and ethnicity on the body—what Demello (1993: 12) calls the "convict body"—as they represent imprisonment and personal, gang, and ethnic affiliation. Cultural politics separate prison tattooing from mainstream tattooing, meaning that even if a prison tattooist is good, he will not be recognized (e.g., published in tattoo magazines), and once released from prison, these artists are rarely hired by tattoo shops.

To be tattooed means the convict becomes part of a community, both their outside community (through tattooed family names and pictures) and inside with *loca* identifying social and ethnic group affiliation. According to Henry Giroux (1992), prison is a cultural borderland where multiple subcultures live on the outskirts of mainstream society. By defining the body, tattoos re-establish the convict's authority over his own body and symbolize his resistance to the prison system, which is vital in an environment where outside identity is stripped away. To not tattoo means social isolation: "Of course there's always the guy that doesn't care what he gets as long as he is identified as one of the fellas, somebody, not some lame nobody" (Demello 1993: 13).

Conclusions

Body art is a visible manifestation of the way humans interpret and depict their bodies and their position in society. Indeed, Schildkrout (2001) calls body art a visual language and suggests that it "can be considered a universal mode of social communication and worldwide medium of expression" (quoted in Peace 2000: 591). In this discussion we examined body painting, piercing, and tattooing. Although not a comprehensive list of body modification and adornment by any means, the examples here clearly indicate that body art, in all its manifestations, is important to humans. The need to express, symbolize, and beautify through body art appears to be an overwhelming human need.

The meaning attached to body art differs from culture to culture. For small-scale cultures, the symbolism most often reflects their group identity, social status, and religious symbolism. Ultimately, their body art is one way to maintain their cultural identity and group solidarity. For youth in Western countries, body art is a sign of resistance and a need to establish a unique identity, as well as membership in a subcultural group. These meanings are particularly evident in a closed and rigid society such as prison. Tattooing in prison creates a common culture, mirroring social hierarchy, and denoting convicts as belonging to communities, while also distinguishing separate ethnic and social groups. Indeed, as Gell (1993) suggests, tattooing provides a portable account of the self.

Through body modification and adornment, the body becomes a theatrical site of display, demonstration, and even resistance that may be read and interpreted by multiple audiences. Thus, body art is performance.

PART IV

GATHERINGS AND POPULAR CULTURE

The need to congregate for social, economic, political, and religious reasons appears to be a universal human behaviour. People come together in churches, synagogues, mosques, and temples to worship; they meet in government houses to choose a political course; they assemble in sports venues to celebrate nationalism; and they visit commercial houses to fulfill material needs. Perhaps the most profound human need is to come together socially in popular gathering places: local coffee shops, *souks* (open-air markets), community halls, bookstores, taverns, cafés, barber shops, playgrounds, sacred circles, movie theatres, ball parks, and central plazas or village courtyards. Today, one of the most interesting yet little understood gathering places is a virtual community on the Internet.

Gathering places are where social networks outside the home or workplace are created, news and gossip is exchanged, and popular culture (singing, dancing, and storytelling) is shared. They are where people go to escape the demands of jobs, spouses, and children; where they can enter into casual conversations with people who hold novel or at least unfamiliar ideas and thoughts; where they can begin a fledgling romance or escape from their identity and responsibilities (Block 2000). Thus, gathering places as an outlet for socialization have become embedded in our everyday popular culture.

Oldenburg (1999) calls gathering places "third places." These third places, as compared to first places (home) and second places (work or school), exhibit certain characteristics. They are neutral spaces that provide a safe haven and anonymity, where people can come and go as they please without having to play host. The rank or status and gender or age of individuals is irrelevant. Indeed, one of the benefits of gathering places is the more or less egalitarian social relationships one enjoys there. Conversation of all sorts is the core activity at a gathering place, while other activities are peripheral to the conversation. Third places are easy to access any time of the day and have "regulars" who set the tone of the place. They are "homely," even shabby, but infinitely comfortable. Their mood is playful, relaxed, and casual, offering a sense of warmth, rootedness, and a shared sense of "home."

Oldenburg (1999) suggests that North America has lost many of its gathering places, first to television and more recently to the computer and Internet. However, Block (2000) more accurately places the blame on city planning; modern North American cities suffer from a dearth of neighbourhood gathering places; even grocery stores are not within walking distance in most suburbs. This trend may be changing; developers and city officials have finally recognized that the absence of gathering places contributes to social isolation and removing them is destroying the social vitality of communities. They are once again building gathering places into the town core. This "new" urbanism is similar to the town squares or commons that were part of early towns (Ghirardini 2001).

A classic example of a gathering place is the coffee house. Coffee houses have been around for several centuries, but they re-emerged with astonishing popularity in the 1990s as North Americans, Europeans, and others looked for "a place away from home." Coffee houses provide a pleasant environment for camaraderie, gossip, and intellectual discourse and promote a sense of community (Hoover 2001). They meet many of the criteria for third places: they are comfortable and often comforting. They cater to a regular clientele, although the demographics of this clientele change through the course of the day: in the morning mothers and babies, retirees, and people who work at home come into the coffee house; in the afternoon, high school youths; and in the evening, young professionals and couples on "coffee dates."

According to legend, the world's first coffee house opened in Damascus in 1530 and quickly diffused through the Ottoman Empire and into Europe by the early seventeenth century. Similar to today, people gathered in coffee houses to play games and share news and gossip. Coffee houses became especially popular in Paris, where figures such as Rousseau and Voltaire frequented them. Today, coffee houses have helped fill in the gap created with the disappearance of Mom and Pop stores, soda shops, and neighbourhood diners.

The Anthropology of Gathering, Socializing, and Celebration

Food plays a pivotal role in gatherings and celebrations. M.F.K. Fisher (1942: 167) once stated, "And with our gastronomical growth will come, inevitably, knowledge and perception of a hundred other things, but mainly of ourselves." Although Fisher was referring to other things than culture per se, it is certainly true that food has meaning and the potential to shape our social bonds with family and community. John Pottier (1999: 7) cautions that anthropology is threatened by a lack of relevance; this certainly holds true in the neglect of food as popular culture. In an extensive review of the literature on the anthropological study of food, Mintz and Du Bois (2002) barely touched on the popular aspects of food and consumption behaviour. Yet, some anthropologists are beginning to address this gap in research.

For Tamara Kohn (2002: 2), "cooking and eating are performances, rich with meaning," and this meaning reveals a great deal about human culture. Anthropologists and other scholars have long studied the symbolic meaning of food and eating, its connection to ritual, and its role in solidifying and distinguishing group membership and identity. They have approached such issues as food and identity through the lens of culture. For example, Ayse S. Caglar (1999) investigated the food preferences of Turkish immigrants living in Berlin and the contemporary marketing of the *doner kebab* (beef roasted on a spit, similar to Middle Eastern shwarmas). It remains a symbol of their Turkish identity and traditions within the context of their struggles to achieve social recognition in Germany (Lien 2002). This study demonstrates the interplay of ethnic identity, class, economics, gender, and political dynamics as played out over the choice of food.

Until recently, anthropologists have failed to consider sports a serious field of study, just as they avoided studying popular culture. Sands (1999: 11) cautions against this narrow perspective, warning that "sports has become both a barometer of social change and a leading agent of social change." Scholars in other fields echo this view, pointing out that sports are integral to our everyday lives, and social scientists who ignore this fact risk overlooking a significant part of human culture. Although anthropologists were quick to study Trobriand cricket as a ritual contest, they ignored similar rituals in Western society. Today, some anthropologists have come to realize that sports are a global phenomenon that have a dramatic impact on the economy of most nations and are of great social consequence to many populations (Stroeken 2002). Indeed, sports can galvanize human passions more than any other dimension of culture. Blanchard (1995) urges anthropologists to examine sports from a holistic perspective: how sports affect or reflect other elements of culture—for example, gender and ethnic stratification—and how sports are affected by culture.

Celebrations among small-scale cultures have always been of interest to anthropologists. This is particularly true of wedding celebrations, where anthropologists have used cross-cultural approaches to examine wedding customs around the world, such as wedding attire and the way this attire creates identity politics and reflects cultural values and ideals. Weddings provide a window into the importance of celebrating familial bonds and creating valuable social outlets.

In this final section, therefore, we will consider three extremely popular reasons for gathering: food, sports, and weddings. Food and its symbolic meaning is important in the study of popular culture. Chapter 8 considers what food means to people and how food can be used to communicate class and cultural identity during its acquisition, preparation, and consumption, first in the cooking of tamales and then at an American barbecue. We will investigate how food consumption and the symbolism of food figures into other aspects of culture, such as socialization and class distinctions. To do so, we will review the ethnographic research of Traphagan and Brown (2002) into eating fast food in Japan and the unconventional but intriguing research of Reed-Danabay (1996) on the well-entrenched French wedding ritual, *la rôtie*.

Some of the earliest ventures in the anthropology of sports studied symbolism and ritual in football (Armstrong & Guilianotti 1997), while other studies (e.g., Back, Crabbe, & Solomos 2001) inevitably turned to issues of identity politics. Both identity and ritual symbolism are addressed in the Stevenson and Alaug (2000) study of football in Yemen. Since any sport is the product of the culture in which it is found, it is also a window into that culture. Indeed, sports can document the values, spirit, and behaviour of a group of people as much as the cultural entities anthropologists traditionally studied. One area of particular interest is sports as an agent of cultural imperialism, as well as a vehicle for cultural resistance. Alan Klein (1995) investigates these dual roles of sports through baseball in the Dominican Republic in Chapter 9.

Of all the subjects of popular culture, wedding rituals have evolved into the most wide-ranging and unique performances, all of which give meaning to the sanctity, responsibilities, and joys of marriage. In Chapter 10, we will explore the roles of gatherings to celebrate marriage as we review the ethnographic research of Natalie Kononenko (1998) on a traditional Ukrainian wedding and conclude with Michael Taft's (2009) ethnographic study of Canadian prairie mock weddings.

Food is essential for human existence not only as an energy source but also for social well-being. One of the most important roles of food is to gather people together and create a sense of community (Ohnuki-Tierney 1997). Coffee houses, restaurants, pubs, even barbecue picnics, all speak to the connection between food and socializing. The global proliferation of food venues reflects a growing prosperity and changing consumption patterns and popular culture. The social importance of food consumption cannot be overstated. In this chapter we will explore eating patterns and the meaning of fast food in Japan through the ethnographic research of Traphagan and Brown (2002).

Food is an important mechanism for acquiring and maintaining social and power relationships. Bourdieu (1984), in his ethnography of France, found a close relationship between aesthetic taste and social class, and posited that taste is often a marker of class. We will address this contention in our investigation of *la rôtie*, a long-standing wedding ritual found in rural France.

Gender is a significant factor in foodways and social allocation. Karen T. Hansen (1999) demonstrated the relevance of gender in studying household dynamics in Zambia. Hansen found that males were always the cooks in colonial households, while in the servants' quarters a woman did the cooking. This gender division of labour has continued into the present despite other changes in domestic service in postcolonial times. The establishment of gender roles and status through food is explored in the cooking of tamales among Tejano migrant farm workers and a barbecue in American suburbia.

The Meaning of Food

Food possesses symbolic meaning for most cultural groups. On New Year's Day, the Chinese eat a vegetarian dish called *jai*. This traditional dish and its ingredients possess several meanings: lotus seeds ensure many male offspring; ginkgo nut, dried bean curd, and black moss seaweed represent wealth; bamboo shoots ensure good fortune and luck. Roast duck is often served at New Year's because red dishes (the duck turns red when it roasts) are the symbol of happiness. The sweetness of sticky rice cakes symbolizes a rich, sweet life, while the layers symbolize increased prosperity and abundance during the coming year. On the other hand, fresh bean curd (tofu) is a taboo food at New Year's because its white colour signifies death and misfortune (Parkinson 2007).

Food may also be a sign of cultural renewal. In Ho Chi Minh City, food stalls magically appear on the sidewalks in front of old shop houses each morning. According to Jackson-Doling (2000), the renewed social and economic vitality in Vietnam revolves around food. The clusters of chairs and tables surrounding a hot cauldron of soup set on an open fire are signs of a cultural renaissance of Vietnam's culinary traditions and the new prosperity the country is now enjoying. In Cuba, folk res-taurants known as *paladare* are small, private restaurants operated from the back of peoples' homes, which not only help Cubans economically but are also rekindling an interest in their ethnic cuisine. These little restaurants offer foreign customers a window into the everyday life of Cubans (Futrell 1998).

Nowadays, eating in commercial restaurants or "dining out" has become an economic mainstay of every urban centre the world over. People gather in cafeterias, sandwich delis, family restaurants, and gour-met dining rooms. The origin of restaurants dates back to the eighteenth century in Europe, when chefs were freed from servitude to the nobility following the French Revolution and began opening their own estab-lishments (Whitaker 2001). In the past, dining out was a sign of status and class—only members of the upper classes patronized restaurants. In North America, the popularity of restaurants grew during Prohibition when stigmas attached to these establishments because of alcohol con-sumption disappeared and families began dining out.

Urbanization and an ever-expanding workforce of both men and women mean that parents are often too busy to prepare home-cooked meals, so the option of dining out has become increasingly popular. During the week, busy office workers congregate at overcrowded, noisy eateries, and businesspeople meet to discuss strategy, woo clients, or even interview for new jobs. Dining out is a social event—people head to res-taurants on the weekend for a family outing, a gathering place for friends, or a courtship venue for young couples. In Europe, on the weekend or after work, plazas are full of friends and families who have gathered at the outdoor restaurants to while away the day.

In Jakarta, Indonesia, *warung* food stalls mushroom in the late after-noon on roadsides, in parking lots, on sidewalks, or in any open space. Passersby stop to choose their food, then sit and enjoy eating it on tempo-rary wooden benches and tables set up around the brightly decorated tents. Each *warung* specializes in a particular menu, usually of regional fare.

Since an economic downturn in 1997, some singers and performers have set up *warung* stalls that attract people who hope they will meet a celebrity. *Warung* may also cluster together in an open field on the weekends and have become popular gathering places for youth. In China, *xiao fanguan,* or little food shops, are very popular because the food is fast and inexpensive. These shops are located on the outside of the bottom floor of apartments in Shanghai; they are little soup kitchens for people without a lot of money, serving noodle or rice dishes. Food has also become increasingly globalized (Mintz & Du Bois 2002). One example of this is the marketing of fast food in Japan that has resulted in an appropriation and naturalization of so-called Western fast food, such as McDonald's.

Traphagan and Brown (2002) conducted an ethnographic study of eating patterns in fast food restaurants in Mizusawa, Japan, to investigate the cultural meaning people attach to such meals. They used a number of approaches in their research: free listing, casual conversations, interviews, and detailed observations of eating habits and social interaction in the restaurants. They found that the proliferation of fast food outlets in Japan has facilitated quality family time and intergenerational communal eating. When a family visits a fast food outlet, the mother orders the food at the counter, while the father and children hold a table and visit with each other. This moment of father-child time is precious and rare in their busy world. The mother then distributes the food and ensures that everyone has something to eat, which is consistent with Japanese culture, where the wife or mother is responsible for feeding the family. Older Japanese rarely eat at foreign fast food outlets like McDonald's, but they frequently visit Japanese ramen noodle shops, which also serve "fast food." There is one notable exception: grandmothers and daughters, daughters-in-law, and grandchildren frequently visit fast food outlets together, thereby fostering an intergenerational intimacy.

Consumption and behaviour patterns at fast food outlets remain distinctly Japanese. Sharing of food is an important Japanese behaviour pattern as a way of strengthening family and friendship bonds. Fries and chicken nuggets are placed in the centre of the table as common family food, similar to the popular tradition of *edamame*—soy beans in their pods placed in the centre of the table to eat before the main meal. Besides common food, members of families and other social groupings take bites out of each other's single burger or share drinks: "We observed one family consisting of a mother, father, and two girls (approximately ages five and seven) who had ordered one hamburger, one large fries, four drinks, four chicken nuggets, and three hot apple pies. Both girls and the mother ate out of the packet of fries. The father and both girls took bites out of the hamburger, though it seemed that the father ate most of it" (Traphagen & Brown 2002: 126). These consumption patterns reinforce emotive bonds in the family and among friends.

The increase in the number and popularity of fast food restaurants in Japan is usually associated with Western cultural imperialism: Japan has the second largest number of McDonald's outlets of any country (Traphagen & Brown 2002: 132). However, Traphagen and Brown believe that this proliferation is the result of changes caused by globalization and modernization processes (e.g., the booming car culture) rather than Westernization per se. Indeed, fast food is not a new phenom- **87** enon in Japan. Street vendors serving roasted sweet potatoes, stand-up noodle shops, take-out establishments, and, more recently, conveyor-belt sushi shops are an integral part of this fast-paced, hard-working society. Conveyor-belt sushi shops offer ready-made, inexpensive sushi placed on saucers that move along a conveyor belt. Customers select their choices as the food passes by and draw self-serve tea from spigots in front of each seat. Fast, inexpensive, and efficient, these outlets are quite popular in Japan. However, by their very nature, conveyor-belt sushi bars offer little opportunity to socialize—customers are watching the conveyor belt for selections and food sharing is at a minimum. These venues run counter to preferred eating patterns by not providing the same opportunities to socialize as other types of fast food venues.

Using free listing and interviews, Traphagen and Brown asked informants to identity what they considered fast food. They found that definitions of fast food outlets varied considerably, becoming increasingly ambiguous when moving from foreign fast food to indigenous Japanese foods. Gender appears to have some influence on whether an outlet is considered fast food: a woman is more likely to visit neighbourhood con- venience stores for pre-packaged lunches, thereby readily identifying these as fast foods, while a man will more likely stop at a stand-up food stall for a snack. Regardless, these informants closely associated fast food with chain restaurants, like McDonald's, and appeared to identify more closely with style of selling than style of food.

The meaning of fast food in Japan has changed over time. When fast food outlets and their foods were first introduced, they were altered to fit Japanese cultural patterns, for example, by adding corn soup and rice burgers to the standard menu. Over time, the foreign foods became naturalized so that it is now considered Japanese food. This also happened with Chinese ramen noodles, which are now considered Japanese. Indeed, fast foods and their outlets have been appropriated and naturalized to the point where many young Japanese think McDonald's and the like are Japanese companies, and they are not considered exotic or foreign.

As one older Japanese put it,

> People like us, of olden times (*furui jidai*), feel strange eating for-
> eign food. We see foods like McDonald's as foreign food. But this
> changes over time. When we were young, ramen was foreign food
> (*shina soba*); it was novel. But today it is Japanese food (*wash-
> oku*). It is no longer an unusual thing. Perhaps twenty years in
> the future McDonald's will be seen as Japanese food and I think
> many younger people perceive of it that way now (Traphagen &
> Brown 2002: 122).

88

Rather than a result of Westernization, this is a response not only to globalization and modernization but the way that fast food restaurants "fit"
with traditional Japanese consumption and behaviour patterns.

In another attempt to understand the meaning of food, anthropologist
Reed-Danabay (1996) studied the symbolism attached to a popular food
ritual or performance known as *la rôtie*. *La rôtie* is a rite of passage into
married life practiced in Lavialle, a dairy-farming community of 18 villages with a population of 350 living in the mountains of Auvergne, France.

According to Mintz and Du Bois (2002), the relationship between
food and the "sacred" can lend itself to the carnivalesque. Here, *la rôtie*
balances the serious nature of marriage with levity and mischief-making,
while also addressing issues of power, status, and identity. In this practice,
local youths interrupt a newly married couple on their wedding night with
a ritual known as *vider le lit* (to overturn the bed). The youths then fill a
decorated chamber pot with champagne and chocolate-coated bananas.
More recently, they may add toilet paper and tampons soaked in tomato
sauce to the mixture in a direct reference to bodily fluids and processes.
The newlyweds drink from the pot and then pass it around amid much
sexual and scatological joking.

La rôtie uses the body (through the symbolic bodily fluids) to express
ideas of inclusion (family and farm) and exclusion (outside the community). The intermingling of bodily wastes in the chamber pot is a metaphor
for the day-to-day physical intimacy, fertility, and economic and social
unity of a Lavialle farm family. The mixture also represents conflicting
messages of taste and distaste. The chocolate and champagne are luxury
foods, and the mixture tastes good, therefore expressing the desirability
of marriage and intimacy. Yet, some of the ingredients, and eating from
the chamber pot itself, are considered vulgar.

From an anthropological perspective, *la rôtie*, with its many meanings—sexual, scatological, class, identity, and ideas of "taste"—presents
an opportunity to ask questions regarding power relations and identity. It expresses local meanings attached to the rite of marriage, the

importance of family as the basic economic and procreative unit, and defines and characterizes the unique local identity of rural Auvergne. *La rôtie* symbolizes the couple becoming members of the community and serves to confirm the official (civil and religious) rituals, while also conferring a new status on the couple. They now represent an intermediary stage between youth and full adulthood, which is gradually attained following the birth of their first child and taking over operation of the farm from their ageing parents.

According to folklorist Arnold Van Geneep (1942, 1946; quoted in Reed-Danabay 1996), *la rôtie* is widespread in rural France, although there are numerous regional variations, using different foods and spices, liquids (bouillon, soup, wine), and containers (clay pots, soup terrines). Yet, all of these rituals use body symbolism. In earlier forms of the ritual, roasted chicken or a dessert made with eggs and cream, symbols of fertility in rural France, were consumed. The phallic chocolate bananas and champagne—the popping of the champagne cork is associated with male orgasm—represent a new emphasis on sexuality rather than fertility in Lavialle.

Auvergne has a reputation among urban dwellers (especially Parisians) as rustic and home to backward peasants lacking any real culture. *La rôtie* participants enter into a dialogue regarding these stereotypes, although they feel self-conscious about the vulgarity of the custom. *La rôtie* also addresses the continuing tensions between rural peasants and urban dwellers by mocking the bourgeois sense of "taste." "Taste" is a marker of class, and in this case, foods of high culture and good taste (champagne, chocolate) are used as a parody or symbolic inversion of food and excrement, high and low culture, and good and bad taste.

Natalie Davis (1975) suggests that festivities and rituals may perpetuate certain values of the community while also criticizing the prevailing political order. *La rôtie* flouts convention and good taste deliberately; therefore, food is used to "create and reinforce social distinction" (Reed-Danaby 1996: 752) and is a form of cultural resistance that both challenges dominant bourgeois culture while also expressing any ambivalence or concerns Lavialle youth may have toward marriage.

Reed-Danabay uses her study of *la rôtie* as an opportunity to chastise anthropologists for their tendency to ignore cultural practices in Western nations. Appadurai (1986: 360) sees this kind of behaviour as "reverse Orientalism," with anthropologists preferring to study small-scale societies over complex Western societies that are not considered "exotic" enough. Reed-Danabay (1996: 759) also berates anthropologists for shying away from distasteful practices, thereby creating a "silence of certain types of knowledge." Most outsiders, including anthropologists, see *la rôtie* as a disgusting ritual and a violation of acceptable codes of taste. This lack of scholarly objectivity reflects cultural and class-based biases toward bodily functions, where even the ethnographic study of such a ritual may be considered in "bad taste."

Despite the narrow-mindedness of some anthropologists, the ethnographic study of *la rôtie* brings to the fore important contemporary anthropological considerations, beginning with the need for anthropologists to expand their ethnographic studies of human culture beyond small-scale, "exotic" cultures, and that includes popular culture. The persistence of cultural diversity in modern cultures suggests that the homogenizing forces of modernization that elicit increasing attention in anthropological and other scholarly works may be overstated. Indeed, practices such as *la rôtie* are a form of cultural resistance to homogenization. *La rôtie*, like most cultural practices, is dynamic; participants have blended older and newer culture forms. This does not mean the custom is disappearing, only that it has adapted according to current issues of power and discourse.

So, as we see, men and women define their identities, gender roles, and status or position through food production, distribution, and consumption (Counihan 1999). The tamale, in myriad ways, demonstrates the symbolic meaning food can hold and the interplay of identity and gender roles in relation to food. Tamales are a popular regional delicacy of the North American southwest, although each locale—Mexico, California, Arizona, Texas, and even Central America—lays claim to the best version (Williams 1984). Each type of tamale owns a rich oral tradition that explains the best preparation and distribution of the food and passes the knowledge on to the next generation. Among Tejano migrant farm workers living at Prairie Junction, Illinois, for six months of the year, the tamale is a highly anticipated treat that marks festive and even sacred events. It also highlights the woman's role as the nurturer of her husband, children, and other kin.

Making tamales is women's work, based on a cooperative association of kin who shop for goods, process, cook, and make the tamales over the course of several days, in the same way Canadian prairie women gather to make perogies. The tamale feast is used to commemorate special events, such as the end of the harvest. A woman may also use the tamale feast to obligate other women she wishes to include in her social support network. In this way, she gains influence as she shares production of food, maintains some control over its distribution, and uses the food to make friends and allies.

The tamale is of ritual importance during the celebration of a girl's fifteenth birthday. As the day approaches, family members gather, and the women begin preparations for the feast, digging barbecue pits, soaking pinto beans, and buying cakes and potato chips from local stores. On the evening of her birthday, everyone in the migrant camp gathers to kiss and congratulate the girl, give her gifts, and feast and dance all night. Beyond the honour bestowed on the girl as she enters womanhood, this festive event binds kin together, recreating obligations and the promise of eventual reciprocity. It also reflects a certain amount of defiance and resistance: despite the desperate economic state of migrant workers' lives, and their domination by others, they can reaffirm their dignity by celebrating life.

The tamale ritually emphasizes a woman's domestic role, while its preparation and sharing reaffirms kin ties. Ultimately, the tamale is a symbol of family and family caring. Tejano women also use foodways to preserve their identity and history, especially when in an alien cultural setting. Thus, the tamale is a symbol of empowerment for migrant women who are otherwise seen as submissive and powerless.

The barbecue was brought to North America by the Taino-Arawak people of Cuba, who cooked their fish on a *barbacoa*. Euro-Americans appropriated the barbecue and naturalized it, and today barbecuing has become a favourite American pastime. Indeed, Laura Dove (n.d.) calls the barbecue an American cultural icon. Historically, barbecues played a central role in church picnics and political rallies, creating a gathering place of like-minded individuals. Today, on any given summer day, it is almost certain that many North Americans will be in their backyard, barbecuing. Indeed, the backyard barbecue has become a seasonal marker: "if the barbecue is lit, it must be summer."

Although most people anticipate the delicious aromas and taste of barbecued meat, in reality it is an informal social occasion more than an eating occasion. Little class distinction is made at barbecues; people from all socio-economic and ethnic backgrounds can meet at a church barbecue, first or fourth of July picnic barbecue, or any other barbecue occasion.

CBC News (2007) calls barbecuing "primal," and they may have a point. Since barbecuing is typically a man's job, the ritual allows men to maintain their male identity while also contributing to meal preparation on the periphery of the domestic sphere. Like the neighbourhood woman who takes great pride in and gains status from her delicious pies, so, too, men gain status from their barbecuing skills. Barbecuing "secrets" are a common theme in recipe sites on the Internet, and competitive barbecues are becoming more common at state fairs and other gatherings. Although not limited to barbecuing, impressing guests with culinary skills, while following well-entrenched "rules," is integral to belonging to a community (Kohn 2002).

Conclusions

Food behaviour is socially and culturally embedded in every society and often possesses special meaning (a whole fish means togetherness in Chinese culture), while other foods have simply become part of cultural heritage and tradition (roast turkey at Christmas in North America). Food may also mean empowerment: a woman who cooks tamales for her husband wields a certain amount of power, while a man known for his barbecuing skills gains status in the community.

McDonald's and the like have been called "global icons." The temptation to "blame" the proliferation of Western fast food restaurants in countries like Japan on Westernization is strong; however, as Traphagen and Brown (2002) point out, fast food resonates with modern Japanese life and culture and meshes with their contemporary social and economic realities.

La rôtie is a popular custom that operates on several levels: injecting some levity into an otherwise serious rite, expressing normal but ambiguous feelings toward marriage and adulthood, and resisting the urban disdain for rural Auvergne people and their seemingly "backward" custom by continuing the ritual. Thus, it reinforces local identity and world view.

According to Mintz (1985), the study of changing consumption patterns can contribute significantly to an anthropology of modern life. Many of these consumption patterns are part of popular culture. Fast food, wedding mischief, and cooking a favourite traditional meal, whether tamales or barbecue, are all parts of popular culture.

"Sports unite by overcoming religious, political, and national barriers."

—President of International Olympic Committee, CBC News Broadcast February 10, 2006.

The roar of the crowd, the smell of hot dogs, and the agony and ecstasy of winning or losing—these are the hallmarks of sports, one of the most all-consuming forms of popular culture. Sports are physical activities that involve skill, competition, and organization, following a set of recognized rules. Early sports evolved to hone subsistence and battle skills and strengthen social networks. Today, sports have become highly competitive, transnational, and commercialized activities that appeal to socially diverse audiences. Football—what North Americans call soccer—is the world's most popular and internationalized sport and takes precedence over even the direst of political events, especially during the World Cup. In the United States, sports have been called "the new American religion," and in Japan, baseball is not a pastime, it is an obsession, and *wa* (team spirit and unity) is all important (Mitgang 1989). Indeed, contemporary sports permeate virtually every aspect of our daily lives and have taken on economic, social, and political roles far beyond that of other leisure activities.

Sports, such as the World Cup, are public performances or spectacles that engage both performers and audience and that elicit emotional responses. Singing or standing to salute the national anthem, for example, is a performance that reinforces and projects an image of unity, the greatness of a nation, and the rightness of its values (Beeman 1993: 380). The symbolism of sports can have a powerful influence on how the audience views the world around them.

Some might wonder why sports are so popular, why the teams that play sports and the fans that support them have become an international phenomenon. According to Stroeken (2002) a team, city, or even nation puts their vitality on the line, and the outcome is never guaranteed. Sporting contests become fascinating to both the participants and the audience because of the lack of control—winning or losing is a matter of chance. This chance element appeals to the magico-realist attitude that has permeated popular culture since the Middle Ages. In other words, spectators and performers revel in the possibility that political and/or economic underdogs may, almost by magic, overcome their subordinate status in the sports arena.

Sports, in their countless expressions, possess multiple meanings and can impact on culture in numerous ways. Like language, sports reflect cultural values and transmit culture from one generation to the next. They can be a voice for expressing nationalism; a forum for playing out political, ethnic, or class rivalries; a tool for re-affirming masculine patriarchy; an influence on race relations; a vehicle for social bonding and group identity; a way to emphasize societal values and religious ritual; and a reflection of changes in society. In this way, sports have helped shape social commentary.

Sports have been called a window on the world. In this discussion, we will examine the role of professional sports in race relations, gender, social equality, identity, nationalism, and cultural resistance. Stevenson and Alaug (2000) suggest that symbolism and ritual found in all sports can be used to convey multiple messages that are interpreted in numerous ways. In their ethnographic research on football in the Republic of Yemen, they found that football helped generate a sense of national identity in the recently unified Yemen state as political leaders formed a national football team and organized a championship tournament to symbolize a message of national unity. Sports have often been accused of being an agent of cultural imperialism, but they may also become a vehicle for cultural resistance and empowerment. We will examine these claims through Alan Klein's (1995) ethnographic research into baseball in the Dominican Republic.

Sports and Its Multiple Meanings

Sports emerged with the advent of urban societies, yet earlier people also filled their leisure time with all manner of games and activities. Tradition plays an important role in the continuity and perpetuation of these ancient sports, some of which have come down through the generations and remain popular today. Archery competitions, for example, are still a favourite sport among Amerindians in Guyana, as are dugout canoe racing and coconut tree climbing. One of the oldest known sports is *ulama*, a ball game played across Mesoamerica for at least 4,000 years. Today, *ulama* is still played in Sinaloa, a western state of Mexico that escaped the intrusion of Catholic missionaries during Spanish colonization (*The Economist* 2004).

The reasons behind the development of early sports are myriad. Hunter-gatherers enjoyed ample leisure time, which presented opportunities for developing games and sports. Most of these were geared toward traditional subsistence strategies and adaptation to their environment. They required little equipment, which fit with the people's migratory lifestyle. The Copper Inuit of north-central Canada practiced foot racing, harpoon and rock throwing contests, ball games, long jump, and wrestling to test their strength and relieve built-up tension. The Chukchi reindeer herders of northern Europe and Siberia practiced lassoing, reindeer sled racing and riding contests, and wrestling, all of which enhanced their strength and endurance and honed their hunting skills (Etylin 2007).

In chiefdoms, with their larger populations and more complex political organization, sports were more elaborate, used more equipment, and had a structured set of rules. They provided social interaction between villages, ways to deal with and solve village rivalries, and opportunities to improve their battle skills. Among the Maori of New Zealand, spear throwing, wrestling, parrying and thrusting, long-distance foot racing, and boxing prepared young boys to become warriors (Best 1934). In Samoa, sports have long played a pivotal role (Dunlap 1951). Swimming and canoe races, diving, and sailing reflected the fact that Samoans took most of their resources from the sea, while land sports like racing, boxing, and wrestling groomed warriors for battle. Beyond perfecting survival skills, these sports involved the entire village, providing opportunities for socialization and reinforcing group unity and support networks.

Sports also reflect the socio-political and religious atmosphere of a nation. In pre-Islamic Turkey, sports were an immensely important component of everyday life (Yurdadon 2003). Games and sports that enhanced warrior skills—for example, archery, horseback riding, cirit (javelin throw), and wrestling—were practiced by both men and women. So important were sports that boys did not receive their public names until they distinguished themselves athletically (Yurdadon 2003, quoting from Lewis 1978). In the Islamic era, sports were greatly influenced by the traditions and moral codes of that religion. Only men were allowed to practice physical activities for leisure purposes. At this time, sports (still cirit, wrestling, archery, and horseback riding) were institutionalized and a few sports clubs were established. In the nineteenth century, Turks were introduced to modern competitive sports, such as basketball and football, by European diplomats, but their sports programs have remained relatively stagnant, in part due to economic limitations.

During colonial expansion, many "pro" sports, such as cricket, baseball, and football, began diffusing to other nations. Most cultures accepted these new sports, modifying them to fit their culture. This is particularly evident in the British game of cricket. Although a product of the colonial era when the British brought this "ritualized warfare" into the nations they colonized, cricket was redefined and took on local meanings (Conway-Long 1998). The game was first introduced to the Trobriand Islanders of Papua New Guinea by British missionaries in the early 1900s (Weiner 1988). The missionaries hoped it would become a substitute for village warfare and sexual "promiscuity" during harvest festivities. To a certain extent they succeeded: cricket did replace warfare between the villages. Yet, Trobriand cricket, with its mock warfare, sexual innuendos, and riotous fun, is hardly recognizable as the staid British version.

96   The Trobrianders naturalized British cricket to suit their cultural needs. Rather than a 12-member team, every man in the village played, sometimes as many as 60 men per side. Each side brought an "umpire" who was expected to control his team but who also performed war magic against the opposing team. The players continued to dress sensually and performed chants and dances at the beginning and end of each inning. Regrettably, European gender restrictions were passed to the Trobriand version of the game. Unlike the harvest dances, where women participated equally, in cricket they were relegated to spectator status, although they still dressed in their provocative finery. Status also played an important role in Trobriander cricket; when a tournament ended, the host village threw a huge feast, thereby acquiring fame and prestige for their generosity. The host team always won the tournament, which at times caused conflict. In 1981, some men burned down village houses in protest over the winning score of a guest team. Yet, for the most part, cricket has become an integral component of Trobriander culture. The creative adaptations Trobrianders made to British cricket have served to reinforce their threatened culture and are symbolic of the way they view British colonialism.

Sports rituals have often been used to promote socio-political messages and play a powerful role in creating national, regional, and ethnic identities (Dyck & Archetti 2003). In 1990 the Yemen Arab Republic and the People's Democratic Republic of Yemen united as the Republic of Yemen. Despite political divisions, financial disparities, and religious and cultural differences, the unified Yemen government was able to socialize its citizens into a new national identity. They accomplished this feat partly through sports.

In the 1970s and 1980s, football in Yemen grew in popularity, attracting large audiences and passionate fans given to outbursts and fights during matches with rival teams. Fans decorated their cars and businesses with team colours as visible markers of their admiration, and conversations focused on upcoming matches between rival clubs. Although popular, Yemen football never became the industry or money-making business it has elsewhere, and European-style football cultures never developed

(Armstrong & Giulianotti 1999). Worldwide, football is a male-dominated sport, and this is true in Yemen, where it is also influenced by male associations and Islamic cultural codes. On the other hand, class is not a limiting factor there; the Ministry of Youth and Sports sets low admission prices and open seating that allows men of any socio-economic class to attend.

Before unification, both Yemen governments encouraged expansion of sports programs and international competition. Football became an emblem of nationalist sentiments. In South Yemen, football was originally a tool used to invite elites and modernists into the colonial sphere, but by the 1920s and 1930s, it promoted solidarity against the British. In the 1950s, it represented Arab and Yemeni nationalism, a trend that continued in the 1960s as clubs supported liberation movements. Following independence in 1967, sports clubs became associated with the state's socialist ideology, and new sports clubs were formed, some in remote regions. In North Yemen, early teams represented modernist ideals, while some in the 1950s opposed theocratic rule. Football became a revolutionary symbol following the 1962 *coup d'état,* and sports clubs that supported the government flourished. In the 1970s, football represented modernization, and new teams were formed in remote areas to integrate rural, culturally disparate regions of the country and to promote national solidarity. In 1969, the first inter-country football match was played, and for many this "football diplomacy" foretold the unification of the country 20 years later (Stevenson & Alaug 2000).

The united Yemeni government employed real and created cultural symbols to mold a national identity. The state organized the first unified football season and formed a national football team with equal representation from both the northern and southern regions of the country. A national championship match known as the Yemen Cup was held to promote a sense of identity with the state and to reinforce symbolically the policies of the government. This sentiment was echoed in an editorial in *ar-Riyadah* newspaper: "One of the positive aspects of the first unified football championship is that it represents the first occasion in which teams from the formerly two Yemens compete in one tournament....This marvellous opportunity comes as a natural extension of the unity of the home land and people" (Stevenson & Alaug 2000: 463). Despite organizational challenges, the nationally broadcast championship game was played as part of the first anniversary celebrations of unification, and football became its symbol.

Sporting spectacles are a natural venue for creating images and imagined communities, operating in a ritual-rich environment that makes people emotionally receptive to messages (Anderson 1991). The sporting events in Yemen were organized to reassure the population that equality

97

in football paralleled equality in state politics: it is easy to imagine a unified nation when there are players on the field competing for their country against another nation (Stevenson & Alaug 2000: 468; quoted in Duke & Crolley 1996: 4). This case shows, then, that football—or any other sport—can and has been used as a forum for promoting socio-political messages.

Baseball is another case in point. Because of its American origins, it has often been accused of being an agent of cultural imperialism. Some indigenous sports have declined or disappeared, especially where Western formal physical education programs have diffused into small-scale cultures (Brownell 1999). Alan Klein (1995) conducted ethnographic field research in the Dominican Republic between 1987 and 1990. He observed the sport from all levels—amateur to professional—interviewed players, and recorded their oral histories. He also gathered archival information, analyzed the sports pages in the country's leading newspaper *Listin Diario,* and conducted a fan survey.

To understand baseball's cultural and ideological importance in the Dominican Republic, readers need to keep in mind three interrelated issues: 1) the United States politically and economically dominates the Dominican Republic; 2) the American major leagues dominate baseball in the Dominican Republic; and 3) the United States increasingly relies on baseball talent from the Dominican Republic (Klein 1995). The United States has employed several means to dominate other countries, and one of them has been baseball (Klein 1995). Indeed, in 1910, A.G. Spalding, one of American baseball's first stars, declared that baseball's function was to "follow the flag around the world" (Spalding 1991: 4; quoted in Klein 1995: 113). According to Calhoun (1987: 228), "Baseball, the grand old American game, is best seen … as an expression of nineteenth-century rural Yankee individualism." Baseball, then, has been viewed as a tool for cultural imperialism. Yet, this is more than a story of political and cultural domination; it is also the story of baseball as a colonial agent that eventually became a source of Dominican empowerment.

American military personnel brought baseball to Latin America, beginning in Cuba in the 1860s. In some countries, such as Mexico, the game was brought by American labourers working on the railway. Although the Americans introduced the game, racial segregation in the United States meant there was little interest in training or hiring Latin American players for American teams because of their skin colour. On the other hand, white and African-American players went to Latin America to play in their leagues. Rogosin (1985) believes this reverse labour migration paved the ideological and cultural way for racial integration in American major league baseball.

Baseball maintained the image of a "gringo's game" throughout the first decades of the twentieth century, even though in Latin America the game was appropriated and became "Latinized." This was a direct response to North American exclusionary policies; Latin American countries developed their own local teams and leagues, as well as a unique playing style known as "wild ball." Latin American baseball players and fans were raucous, as was their music. They had an artistic flair for smart moves and hustle. According to Klein (1995), the tempo and rhythm of the game meant line drives, speedy base running, and one-handing short stops were an important component of the game, unlike American players' emphasis on brute force. Cool Papa Bell, a player for the Pittsburgh Crawfords of the Negro Leagues in the 1930s and 1940s remarked, "All through my career, we put emphasis on what I call trick baseball. We played with our heads more than with our muscles…I think the reason we had so much success against major leaguers was the difference in styles, the major leaguers waited around for somebody to hit a home run, while we worked on the strategy and the fundamentals" (Bankes 1991: 113; quoted in Klein 1995: 115).

Following desegregation in baseball, players from the Dominican Republic were drafted into the American major leagues to cover the looming talent shortage, caused by the preference of African-American athletes for American football and basketball over baseball. Academies were established in the United States and Canada in the 1970s to hone Dominican talent. Successful players became national heroes in the Dominican Republic, and many returned each winter to play in their homeland. However, by the 1980s, with free agency and greatly increased salaries, most Latin American players stopped playing in their home country, which resulted in declining attendance at games. This mining of Dominican talent inevitably led to the underdevelopment of the country's own baseball.

The exploitation of Dominican sports heroes and decimation of local baseball leagues parallel American economic domination of the Dominican Republic and mirror the role of Canadian and American multinationals in that country. Yet, to Latin American men, baseball offered an economic opportunity. It became very easy for young men to view the sport as their economic salvation and an escape from poverty, and the numbers are significant: Klein (1995) estimates that 1,000 young Latin men earn a living in baseball.

Culturally, baseball was a conduit through which Dominicans grew fascinated with the American way of life and its fashion, music, movies, and of course, sports. Consumption of American products became widespread. Throughout this book, we have raised the question of whether the diffusion of popular culture has influenced other cultures and other popular cultures. In the Dominican Republic the desire for all things American created a form of self-loathing and repudiation of ethnic origins; people accepted the notion that Anglo-Americans were superior to Dominicans and that all things Dominican were inferior in quality and desirability. Although the Dominicans appropriated and naturalized baseball, the negative effects of American baseball in the Dominican Republic are hard to ignore.

There is another side to this equation—nationalism. Nationalism on a general level promotes one's own culture and nation over others (Anderson 1991), thereby countering the overvaluation of a foreign nation and reducing self-loathing. This is where baseball was transformed from an agent of cultural imperialism to a vehicle for cultural resistance and empowerment. In the case of the Dominican Republic, the media, such as *Listín Diario,* took a pro-Dominican, anti-American nationalist stance over sports, although other sections of the paper ignored the economic crisis brought on by multinationals and foreign investors. The fact that Dominican players and other Latinos were mainly responsible for the success of the American major leagues was regularly expounded. During the summer season, the Dominican press focused on Dominican players in the major leagues, heralding Dominican nationalism and ignoring other aspects of the game, such as the final score. In the winter season, the press "gringo-bashed," blaming the declining attendance at local games on the major leagues' theft of the Dominican's best players. The media, then, used sports to express the growing resentment of Dominicans against American hegemony (Klein 1995).

In the streets, Klein found that nationalism was everywhere. In an experiment, Dominicans were asked to choose between baseball caps, one Dominican, one American. Seventy-eight per cent (128 out of 164) selected the Dominican hat. When asked why, the comments were clearly nationalist: "I'm Dominican, I'm not some gringo who wears a Dodgers hat." Klein found that upper-class Dominicans were more likely to choose an American hat, a predictable result given that they were more likely benefiting from the foreign presence (Klein 1995: 127). Nationalism, through sport, has the power to counteract American cultural hegemony, and this is exactly what has happened in the Dominican Republic.

Equality in Sports

Sports often reflect the values of a group of people and, in turn, how these values change over time, and this includes removing socio-economic, gender, racial, and ethnic barriers. Gender is embedded in sports, and there is little doubt that most sports are androcentric. Commercials during sporting events exemplify male imagery—the hardworking, beer swilling manly man—a powerful agent for promoting ideals of masculinity (Conway-Long 1998). Even in indigenous cultures, such as in Samoa, where gender equality is more evident, sports are embedded with male imagery and masculine ideals, such as toughness. Interestingly, at the local level, and especially among children, there is a higher level of female participation in sports, and in some cultures older women, freed from childcare responsibilities, also participate more often. As an exception, Mesoamerican *ulama* does not present a gender barrier for women—both men and women play the game. Archaeological and ethnographic data suggests this was so in pre-Columbian days as well, and women likely only ceased playing during the active missionary/colonization era, then resumed the game some 200 years ago (Noverr 2001).

One of the defining moments in baseball history occurred on April 15, 1947, when Jackie Robinson became the first African-American professional baseball player. He became a role model for all athletes and paved the way for future generations of African Americans and other visible minority athletes. Robinson endured a great deal of abuse in the early years from his Brooklyn Dodgers teammates, some of whom started a petition to have him fired; pitchers who deliberately threw balls right at him; bench jockeys who ordered him to carry their bags or shine their shoes; and "fans" who mocked him, wearing mops on their heads or sending him death threats (Aaron 1999). Yet, with dignity and resolve, Robinson persevered. In doing so, he forced the sporting public to finally deal with segregation in sports and offered a glimmer of hope that, at least in that arena, racial barriers were disappearing. Today, African Americans, Hispanics, and numerous other visible minorities play in professional sports, due in part to the bravery and character of Jackie Robinson.

The struggle to remove racial and ethnic barriers did not end with Jackie Robinson; discrimination in sports is still prevalent, although today it is often couched in rules and issues of safety that make it difficult to stop the discrimination. In April 2007 young Muslim women were barred from wearing their *hijab* (Muslim traditional headscarves) while participating in a Tae Kwon Do tournament in Montreal. The team withdrew from the tournament in protest. Was this discrimination? The officials say no, it was a matter of safety, and the official rules forbid the wearing of anything under the helmet. Yet, the rule seems to be haphazardly applied—the same team competed a year earlier with no problem (Stastna 2007). Other Muslim women have experienced the same problems. In February 2007 a girl was barred from a soccer tournament for wearing the *hijab*, a symbol of Muslim faith and cultural identity. Cultural inclusion versus entrenched and exclusionary sporting rules is an issue with which sports officials will have to deal in the coming years.

Conclusions

What do sports mean? This is a question impossible to answer succinctly. Sports contain multiple messages and meanings, and these meanings change over time. Although the reasons offered in this discussion all play a significant role in why sports are so popular, we should not ignore their entertainment value. Sports are fun to watch and play; the excitement and suspense of an unscripted outcome, and the awe in watching a skilful performance are valuable components. Unlike other forms of entertainment, such as movies, the outcome of a sports competition is unknown (Mandelbaum 2004). Yet, there are clearly identifiable rules and a coherence seldom found in real life that appeal to our need for security.

Despite criticisms, sports do serve a valuable role in society. They are not frivolous, expensive pastimes; rather, sports allow people to express themselves emotionally, create a common bond between fans even if only during the game, allow exuberant socializing, build on civic and national pride, and remind people of their patriotism during times of crisis. Sports, then, are a vital component of popular culture, steeped in tradition, ritual, and social commentary that impact greatly on the other elements of culture.

What do a Ukrainian *devich vechir,* Indian *mehndi* party, Egyptian *zaffa* march, Moroccan *beberiska* painting, Maori *powhiri* welcome, Chinese tea ceremony, and prairie mock wedding have in common? They are all wedding rituals deeply embedded in our popular culture. The pageantry, traditions, and ritual attached to the wedding ceremony and to related celebrations in the years to come are popular performances that express the global significance of marriage. Indeed, Otnes and Pleck (2003) suggest that weddings have become a worldwide consumer ritual that continues to increase in popularity.

Weddings are rites of passage that symbolically transform adolescents into adults with adult responsibilities. Rituals performed at a wedding ceremony may be as straightforward as the bride and groom eating cooked yams the bride's mother has prepared, as is the custom among Trobrianders of Papua New Guinea, or as elaborate as the days and weeks of ritualized wedding preparations, feasting, and parties involving an entire Ukrainian village. Wedding ritual, then, is performative spectacle that may transform public and private spaces into public displays of success.

In most cultures, wedding rituals are both sacred and secular, a meshing of religious symbolism, consumer culture, and romanticism, which often makes for difficulty in separating the economic, social, political, and religious reasons for wedding rituals from the popular. Wedding rituals are dynamic and given to some hybridity, with modern weddings incorporating some ancient traditions, modifying others, and adopting new, often foreign practices to create glocalized weddings. This is evident in contemporary Japanese weddings that combine traditional Shinto rituals with Western components such as three-tiered, frosted wedding cakes, white wedding gowns, and "talent-show-like receptions" (Edwards 1989: 169).

Marriage itself is a universal pattern of human behaviour that serves several important socio-cultural functions: creating a conjugal couple and a family unit for raising children; defining gender roles and expectations within a particular culture; and symbolizing the joining together of two families, thereby increasing a social and perhaps economic network. It is also one way to establish a household, the basic economic unit from which many economic activities flow. Thus, marriage as a cultural institution provides a way of meeting some of our basic human needs. The importance of marriage is symbolized in wedding performances, such as the complex rituals in a traditional Ukrainian wedding.

Ukrainian weddings are steeped in tradition, symbolism, and popular rituals. Anthropologist Natalie Kononenko (1998) observed several such weddings in villages in Central Ukraine in the Cherkas'ka and Kyivs'ka oblasts, and the following description is taken predominately from her observations and ethnographic research.

Although the weddings were contemporary, Kononenko noted some behaviour that suggested cultural renaissance and the revival of village traditions; for example, some brides had returned to wearing embroidered Ukrainian dresses (*vyshyvka*) and wreath headpieces (*vinok*) rather than the lavish white gowns appropriated from the West in previous years. This trend ran counter to the white-wedding-dress global phenomenon. Some brides have blended (hybridized) the two traditions, wearing a white gown and veil for the ceremony and a *vysyvka* for the reception.

Extended family relationships are of paramount importance in rural Ukraine: the joining of two people in marriage is also the joining of two families. This perspective is evident in the wedding ritual, which begins with a formal engagement. The groom, with several friends or respected community elders along for support, visits the bride's home to ask her parents' permission to marry. Betrothal gifts are exchanged: the groom's party offers a bottle of *horilka* (homebrew), and the bride drapes the elders with ritual towels (*rushnyky*). Both parties offer loaves of bread to the other, symbolizing acceptance of the engagement and the joining of two families. In a contemporary adaptation, the engagement is usually a formality; the bride and groom have already courted and privately agreed to marry.

The offering of bread continues to be an important symbol during ensuing celebrations; a special bread called *korovai* (wedding cake or bread) is prepared. A party (*devich vechir*) is held where the bride bids farewell to her childhood and, with her friends, makes a *hiltse* from pine branches, a ritual tree that will sit on the head table during the reception and symbolize the fun and joy in marriage. On the morning of the wedding, the bride and groom, accompanied by a bridesmaid (*druzhka*) and best man (*boiaryn),* walk through the village offering ritual bread (*shyshka*) and summoning their wedding guests.

The actual wedding ceremony is the low-key signing of a civil document, although there may be a church service the next day. Following the signing, the bride and groom are separated, returning to their own parents' houses for a meal, then the groom heads to the bride's house where he takes part in a comedic drama of sorts: he is refused passage inside the bride's home until he pays a ransom (usually some *horilka* and a little money). The ritual resistance over, the groom is allowed to join his bride at the table where another elaborate meal is served to the guests, and the wedding cake (*korovai*) is cut and distributed. The couple then return to the groom's house for more food, *horilka,* speeches, gift-giving, and dancing. The bride's family may also formally present the bride's wedding chest, with linens and other goods the bride has been collecting for years. During a final meal at the groom's house, the groom's wedding cake is cut and shared with the wedding guests. The next morning the bride and groom enjoy a ceremonial breakfast, which may also include ritually displaying proof that the bride was a virgin. The emphasis during the festivities appears to be on family feasting. Food at a Ukrainian wedding is of paramount importance; celebratory meals are opportunities to enjoy bountiful food and imbibe great quantities of alcohol amid many toasts to the health and happiness of the new couple.

Up to this point, the rituals have contained at least an element of solemnity, despite consuming large quantities of homebrew. The next stage is more about fun, mischief, and merriment: stealing chickens, then cooking and eating them at the groom's house; playing tricks on those who had returned to their daily tasks, such as taking gates off their hinges; hiding equipment; and cross-dressing or wearing costumes. Kononenko witnessed an individual dressed in a doctor's outfit, performing an entrance ritual—anyone wanting to enter a house had to have their temperature taken with a broom stick. Several men, pretending to be horses, pulled the parents of the bride and groom through the streets in a decorated cart, with other villagers following behind. They stopped periodically and demanded *horilka* to keep going. Anyone they encountered was expected to offer a small gift to the newlyweds. At the river's edge, the parents were dumped into the water—a form of water ritual—and soon everyone present was soaking wet.

A Ukrainian wedding performance articulates several messages. The first, and most obvious, is the joining together of two young people and the creation of a new family unit with the potential to create the next generation of villagers and, by extension, welcoming the new couple into the community as adults. The wedding rituals also link the bride's and groom's families in a system of mutual support. They honour the parents of the couple, who have raised their children to become productive members of the community. Although the wedding is considered a sacred event, the merriment serves to balance this sacredness, and the wedding rituals bring the community together to socialize.

During the Soviet era, officials attempted to ban some of the popular customs, especially cross-dressing, but the practices persisted. Kononenko (1998: 5) rightly points out that any solemn occasion needs a bit of frivolity to act as a balance—"sealing the serious rite with the magic of laughter." Indeed, the water ritual is a rite of intensification, since water ensures crop fertility. Thus, the traditional Ukrainian wedding is an important social event that brings together families and eases the hardships and rigours of life, at least for a time.

The social importance of wedding rituals may even be reflected in subsequent celebrations, such as the little known but highly popular prairie mock wedding. "What does it mean to marry a farmer and become a farm wife?" This is the question addressed In the mock wedding, a dramatic satire of a typical prairie wedding celebration. Although mock weddings are found in several Ukrainian-Canadian prairie communities, the custom is region-specific rather than ethnic-specific; people of other ethnic groups also hold them. The roots of mock weddings go back to nineteenth-century Tom Thumb and womanless weddings in eastern North America, although today they are found mainly in Canadian prairie communities. Contemporary prairie mock weddings are localized and customized to fit the honoured couple and the cultural mores of the region, whereas in eastern Canada, where some mock weddings are also held, the ritual tends to be more standardized.

Anthropologist and folklorist Michael Taft (2009) calls the mock wedding a ritual within a ritual because it is usually held as part of a wedding anniversary celebration, most commonly for the twenty-fifth. The anniversary party is often held at a local community hall and involves a great deal of eating and drinking; gift-giving; grandiose speeches, often of the "roast" variety; dancing to the local band; and visiting with friends, relatives, and neighbours.

One of the most common elements of a mock wedding is cross-dressing. Male cast members don the wedding costumes of women—dresses, high heels, and wigs—carry bouquets (usually weeds), and wear exaggerated make-up. The female cast members wear men's clothing—suits, ties, and shoes—slick their hair back with grease, and may sport fake mustaches or beards. At the mock wedding I attended in 1973, the rather corpulent male cast members were naked from the waist up. Female faces were drawn on their rotund bellies so that when the men flexed their stomach muscles, the faces made funny expressions that greatly added to the frivolity of the evening.

Taft (2009: 374) has found that although prairie men are proud of their manliness, a "reverse machismo" is also at work in this cross-dressing. These men are so secure in their masculinity that they willingly give up their identity and dignity to cross-dress. They ham it up for the ceremony, posing and clowning around, and mimicking so-called feminine traits such as "mincing, blushing, and speaking in a falsetto voice." They often act in a bawdy manner, scratching inappropriately and adjusting their stuffed bras and tight girdles. At the same time, these female impersonators ensure that the audience recognizes their masculinity by strutting and flexing their hairy muscles and generally swaggering around in an exaggerated male manner. All of this behaviour is designed to assert their "maleness."

Besides this cross-dressing, the mock wedding ceremony is full of sexual innuendoes, tomfoolery, and, despite a script, some hilarious ad-libbing. The wedding procession enters the hall to the sounds of whistles, catcalls, jeers, and a great deal of laughter. The "couple" takes their place in front of a *faux* minister, surrounded by bridesmaids, groomsmen, and parents. Often the "father" of the bride is carrying a shotgun. "Vows" are exchanged, the minister reading from a catalogue or *Playboy* magazine. One common tradition of this ceremony, when the minister asks if anyone can show why the couple cannot wed, is the frantic appearance of a girlfriend who is either made up to appear pregnant or carrying a baby. The following is an eye witness account of a mock wedding for close relatives:

> The mock wedding was hilarious. The preacher, who was a family friend, stumbled over the wedding vows; the bridesmaid bent over in the middle of the ceremony to adjust her stockings and the groom brought out a large hoop earring for the ring. It was almost three inches across and the bride was almost able to fit it over his wrist. When the preacher said, "if anyone objects, speak now...," my grandfather stepped out from the corner of the house, carrying his shotgun (Alward 1999).

The couple is eventually pronounced husband and wife, and a kiss is exchanged, which often devolves into a wrestling match.

The role of each character is noticeably stereotyped: the weeping mother carries a roll of toilet paper to dab at her dripping eyes; the father of the bride (see shotgun above) is gruff and demanding; and the ring-bearer carries a teething ring, washer, or some other form of ring. The minister often carries a jug of homebrew and takes an occasional drink. The bride and groom tend not to be as stereotyped; rather, their behaviour is a caricature of the real couple's personalities. At one mock wedding, during the vows the minister asked the groom if he will buy his chickens rather than steal them from the neighbours, a reference to a real event in the groom's life. The bride is often taken to task regarding her cleaning or cooking abilities, or some embarrassing moment in the couple's married life is mentioned.

The production of a mock wedding is the responsibility of a producer-director, usually a woman from the community, who writes the script, locates all the props and costumes, and chooses cast members. Like the master of ceremonies at a wedding reception, the director must find funny and embarrassing stories to tell about the couple. Yet, this producer faces some restrictions on how far she can go in revealing the couples' private life. For example, in one mock wedding ceremony that Michael Taft (2009) encountered, the "father and the shotgun" sequence was removed because the whole community knew the woman had been pregnant at the time of the wedding.

The mock wedding is a commentary on the ambiguous yet rigid gender roles of prairie women living and working on family farms. There is a great deal of conflict between the feminine roles of women and the actual farm work they must do in order to survive economically—driving a grain truck or combine during harvest time, slaughtering chickens, and maintaining the farm accounts. All of these tasks are considered men's work, yet women find themselves performing these duties, even though in other ways they are expected to adhere to traditional female gender roles by cooking, cleaning, and caring for the children.

Women impersonating men in these mock wedding ceremonies are not as obvious in their role-playing. However, women do have a message to send: "as farm wives, we are both women and men at the same time." Even the "vows" address the duality of a farm wife's role: "Do you promise to clean the slaughterhouse mess and not love and honour your husband any less?" or "Do you promise from harvest to harvest to serve him with coffee and cake?" Mock weddings provide women with an opportunity to express their frustrations with conflicting domestic roles. Indeed, the vows speak for the women. Through performance, then, the women articulate these frustrations to the audience and to each other. For the men, taking on the roles and dress of women gives them the opportunity to experience, at least for an evening, the ambivalence and burden of having to live two roles.

Like the original wedding ceremony, mock weddings serve many of the same purposes. They are an opportunity for isolated prairie farm families to socialize. From babies to elders, the people of these communities gather together for fun, fellowship, and entertainment while also honouring the celebratory couple. This is also an opportunity for young people to meet each other and perhaps establish a courting relationship. The anniversary is an opportunity for friends and relatives from far away to come together at a reunion of sorts. The frivolity of a mock wedding ceremony lightens the mood and releases inhibitions, and for a time the people forget their troubles and have fun together. Verardi (2000) found that the mock wedding changes the sacred wedding ritual into a secular celebration. Using humour, satire, and bawdy behaviour during the mock wedding performance allows female participants to call attention to their frustrations, while the men "walk in their shoes" and experience some of the duality of a prairie farm wife's gender roles.

Conclusions

On the surface, wedding rituals are performed to legalize and sanctify a marriage, but the meaning of a wedding goes much deeper regardless of the culture or the ritual. Weddings symbolize the joining of two people and the creation of a new family and household that may produce the next generation and thus perpetuate the continuation of a lineage. The wedding preparations, ceremony, and celebration all provide opportunities to acknowledge this union. So, too, the wedding rituals acknowledge the joining of two families through their children. In many cultures, this is at least as important as the marriage between two people.

The celebrations are also an important familial and community social outlet, one that binds groups together and acknowledges the interconnection of members. In the case of mock weddings, the celebration recognizes a successful marriage and is a renewed testament to the union and the importance of being part of a community. These rituals, although cherished, are given to change, adopting new forms, while also retaining traditional elements; hence, most wedding rituals today are hybrid to one degree or another. Wedding ceremony, ritual, and performance, then, are an important component of human culture, although, as we have seen, it is often difficult to separate the popular from the sacred.

Writing this book became for me a fascinating journey of discovery. I have argued that popular culture is the culture of everyday life and that this is true of *all* cultures, not only Western societies. My opinion has not changed since undertaking this research. Yet, I have repeatedly encountered people who consider only Western pop music, pop art, pop fiction, and entertainment programs on film and television popular culture. There is a definite sense that this kind of culture is fun and interesting but also slightly inferior to other "serious" forms of culture, such as symphonic music, classical art, and literary fiction. I have endeavoured to introduce case studies of popular culture from outside this narrow definition, such as the champagne and chocolate wedding ritual in rural Auvergne or the making of Ukrainian *pysanky*.

The scope of pop culture is mind-boggling; for instance, recently a commentator on *Good Morning America* identified using models in political ads as a form of pop culture. Pop culture is everywhere; it is embedded in every culture, in every cultural institution. It surrounds us and defines us, and has always done so. Pop culture, like the systems of culture, is integrated—dining out encompasses fashion, music, ethnic food, and car culture. A love of sports also means collecting sports memorabilia, gathering at sports venues, body art, music, vacationing, and so on. The prophetic words of Browne and Browne (2001)—that it may not be possible to fully understand popular culture, not our own or any other—came back to haunt me on several occasions.

Popular culture means many things to many people, and to attempt to analyze it may be a disservice to its myriad forms. Popular culture is always in a state of flux, constantly evolving and generating new forms—that is its nature and part of its attraction. It also seems that new popular culture, regardless of what generation we are looking at, is constantly struggling to find its place and gain some respect.

Many of the insights presented in *Pop Culture* are based on my own experiences—a chance conversation with colleagues, a night out on the town, or a media presentation. At other times, I have drawn on the ethnographic research of other scholars to investigate certain types of popular culture. Both avenues of research have served to expand my understanding of its multifaceted nature and meaning. In this Conclusion, I will summarize some of the insights, impressions, and experiences gained in the two years of researching this book. The Internet has proven a boon, since it is online that popular culture is acknowledged, embraced, and accepted for what it is, rather than in academic presentations that can theorize the heart out of anything.

Of increasing concern to me and many others is the rapid diffusion of Western popular culture to other regions of the world. I have only to open the windows of my apartment in Cairo to hear Western rock 'n' roll blaring from car stereos as evidence of the impact Western popular culture is having on youth in other cultures. Yet, I have also noticed that local popular culture—Arab music, dress, food, and television programs—are still valued. Is there room for both? I happen to think so.

The processes of creolizing or hybridizing various forms of popular culture are not as dire as many think, nor is it a new phenomenon. Historically, culture change and hybridity nearly always occurred whenever cultural groups came into close contact. What *is* of concern is the rapidity with which these changes are occurring today. Modern telecommunication and transportation systems diffuse new ideas and behaviours in weeks and months now, rather than years. Cultural groups are infinitely adaptable, but they need time to make and adjust to changes, and this rapid influx of foreign influences may prove challenging to some local popular cultures. Even here, though, I have some qualifications. My research has led me to believe that highly valued, tightly embedded popular culture is likely safe, perhaps not from some hybridity but certainly from loss. People tend to be highly selective and adopt only those elements of another culture that they see value in or that they prefer over their own. In this regard, remember the discussion in Chapter 1 of changing bridal customs in China (see page 38).

"Global youth culture" is an interesting concept. As with most culture change, it is the youth who seem to embrace new ideas, new material goods, and new popular culture most readily. Indeed, some critics have even accused global youth culture of being an agent for Western ethnocentrism and cultural imperialism. Others see it as a medium for positive change, creating a hybrid, cosmopolitan generation that epitomizes many voices, many cultures, and many styles. Exposure to myriad cultures and world views has given global youth a range of new opportunities to question, shape, and adopt cultural ideas and attitudes they admire, while rejecting repressive or reactionary attitudes that may harm their culture. Global youth cultures have the power and voice to express their political views that previous generations never enjoyed.

I have also encountered a great deal of concern over globalization through multinational corporations. The massive advertising campaigns inundating foreign markets cannot help but have an impact on local popular culture. We need only look at McDonald's as an example. During my roamings through Middle Eastern and Asian countries, I have never had to look for a McDonald's—one is always right there, and incredibly busy, with people fighting to reach the counter. Is it because the food tastes good? Or is it because McDonald's has become a cultural icon, a symbol of Western culture that others want to adopt? Doubtless, this trend is having an impact on traditional food outlets, but again, those foods highly valued are only moving over, not disappearing.

112   Popular culture has endured a great deal of criticism regarding its commodification and over-commercialization. I find it difficult to take this criticism seriously. All that we produce, believe, and value has some "price" attached to it, and I challenge anyone to come up with an example of some component of culture where this is untrue. Yet, it is important to recognize that commercialization of popular culture can have an impact on the form it takes and its long-term stability.

And now back to anthropology. In a caustic, yet perceptive, critique of anthropology's myopic view, Davis (1997: n.p.) chides: "Anthropology is only anthropology if it is done very much abroad, in unpleasant conditions, in societies which are very different from the ethnographer's native habitat, very different from the sort of place where he [sic] might go on holiday." This narrow-sightedness has stymied anthropology's growth for many years and has kept the field from remaining relevant in today's dynamic global world. Although some of the case studies in *Pop Culture* were taken from non-Western cultural groups, it is important to recognize that all of these cultures are part of the modern global culture, as is the West. The study of Western pop culture is no less important than that of a small-scale culture. Fortunately, a new generation of anthropologists is moving into positions of authority, and many of them recognize that to remain relevant they must study what is relevant to *people,* and this most definitely includes pop culture.

GLOSSARY

androcentrism: Male-centredness.

anthropology: The study of human-kind in all times and places. Anthropology is usually divided into four major sub-disciplines: biological anthropology, archaeology, linguistic anthropology, and socio-cultural anthropology. Biological anthropologists study humans as biological organisms. Archaeologists seek to reconstruct human behaviour and lifeways in the past. Linguistic anthropologists study how people use language to interact with each other and transmit culture. Socio-cultural (also referred to as cultural or social anthropology) anthropologists study human behaviour in contemporary cultures.

appropriation: The adoption of a cultural element, such as a musical style, from one cultural group by another.

artefacts: Material objects that have been made by humans, that can be removed from a site.

artistic expression: The expression of ideas, values, and beliefs through works of art.

authenticity: True to origins.

body adornment/body modification: Decoration (tattoos, jewellery, painting) or modification (piercings, cuttings, branding) of the human body. Acceptable body adornment varies from one culture to another and from one generation to another:

body art: Decoration on the body, such as painting, tattooing, piercings, and hairstyles.

body painting: Pigments applied to the body in various designs, each symbolizing certain desired characteristics or outcomes (e.g., fertility).

body piercings: The practice of puncturing or cutting a part of the human body, often for the purpose of creating an identity or as a fashion statement.

border markers: Symbols (e.g., tattoos) that create divisions or separations between classes, genders, ethnic groups, and so on.

censorship: The banning or stymieing of various media content, such as expletives (e.g., in rap music) or sexually graphic content (e.g., pornography) from the public's view.

class/social class: A recognized category or ranking within a stratified society based on achieved status. Open class systems allow for social mobility (up or down in class), while closed systems, such as castes, do not allow for social mobility.

colonialism: When one nation dominates another, through occupation (colonies), administration (military presence), and control of resources (foreign corporation), thereby creating a dependency.

communication: Messages passed between individuals that are mutually understood. May contain elements of non-verbal communication (body language, paralanguage, tone), as well as spoken words.

community: A shared, fixed territory, such as a neighbourhood, but also relationships and activities based on familiarity and interdependence; may be a social space rather than a physical space.

conspicuous consumption: To consume and/or display material wealth in excess of normal needs in order to gain prestige; for example, one person occupying a mansion and owning numerous luxury vehicles.

consumerism: The act of consuming resources; usually refers to purchasing these resources through the market economy.

consumption: The expenditure or using of resources.

counterculture: Movements within a culture that run contrary to mainstream norms of behaviour. They are designed to stimulate cultural change or at least offer alternative lifestyles.

creolization: The blending of cultural elements, such as musical styles.

cross-cultural comparison/perspective: An approach whereby one aspect of a culture (e.g., ritual) is compared in many cultures in order to develop hypotheses or theories about human behaviour.

cultural diversity: Analogous with ethnic diversity, meaning that several cultural groups occupy a given region or society, while continuing to display distinct features and behaviours.

cultural flow: The diffusion of cultural elements from one culture to another, usually through prolonged contact.

cultural icons: Tangible symbols of cultural elements, values, and practices; for example, the celebrity of Elvis Presley.

cultural identity: The culture to which an individual feels they belong, based on their upbringing, residence, heritage, customs, and language.

cultural imperialism: Promoting a nation's values, beliefs, and behaviour above all others. Often associated with the Western world's inundation of other cultural groups through technology, beliefs, and ways of living via the media, missionism, the military, education, and, in particular, economic power.

cultural pluralism: A society that possesses more than one recognized cultural group that demonstrates different ways of living. Also known as multiculturalism.

cultural production: The creation of cultural elements that are used for some purpose such as cultural resistance.

cultural relativism: The principle that each culture and its practices is unique and valid in its own right and must be viewed within the context of that culture, not that of outsiders. Anthropologists use the relativistic approach to avoid judging or interfering with the behaviour of people in the cultures they study.

cultural renewal: Initiatives to revive or maintain cultural elements.

cultural resistance: Resisting domination of a culture from outside forces through avenues such as sports nationalism.

culture: The shared ideals, values, and beliefs that people use to interpret, experience, and generate behaviour. Culture is shared, learned, based on symbols (e.g., language), and integrated.

115

culture change: The process of changing the behaviour, technology, and beliefs within a culture. Culture change is inevitable and happens in all cultures, albeit at different rates. Change may come about through internal changes (e.g., invention, innovation) or external changes (e.g., diffusion, acculturation).

cyberanthropology: The anthropological study of humans interacting through Internet environments and of the social communities that have developed online.

cyberspace: A conceptual framework of people, places, and information linked via the Internet. Cyberspace exists without time, space, or physical restraints (Scott 1998); a conceptual space that enables people to conduct communication, develop human relationships, and manifest wealth and power (Rheingold 1996).

diffusion: The transmission, spreading, or borrowing of cultural components from one culture to another culture. The most likely cultural components to be diffused are technology, while belief systems are much less likely to diffuse without some form of missionism.

digital divide: Divisions based on age, gender, socio-economic status, location, and so on, between those who commonly use the Internet and those who do not have access to it.

discrimination: Distinctions made about people based on gender, age, sexual orientation, disabilities, or ethnic identity that result in differential access to resources and opportunities.

emic perspective: Viewing a cultural feature or system from the cultural members' perspectives as compared to the anthropologist's perspective (etic).

enculturation: The process of learning our culture, usually through transmission from one generation to the next.

ethnic group: A group of people who identify themselves as an ethnic group based on a shared ancestry, cultural traditions and practices, and a sense of a common history, thereby distinguishing them from other ethnic groups.

ethnic identity: The identity we possess based on our membership in an ethnic group.

ethnography/ethnographic research: The major method of anthropological fieldwork involving the process of collecting first-hand descriptive data on a culture. The end result—ethnography—is a written description of the people and their way of life.

exploitation: The systematic use of resources or people for political and or economic gain.

family: A vague and complex term that means many things to many people, but generally is defined as people who consider themselves related through kinship. There are two major forms of family: nuclear, containing parents and children; and extended, containing several generations (e.g., grandparents, aunts and uncles, and cousins), as well as parents and children. Today, single-parent families (only one parent in the household) are becoming an increasingly significant demographic.

folk art: Artistic endeavours by ordinary people within small communities. Usually not widely distributed nor possessing extrinsic value.

gathering places: Those places where people gather for socializing, entertainment, and various other activities (e.g., local pub or café).

116

gender: A cultural construct that gives us our social identity, status, and roles in society. We learn our gender identity and roles through enculturative forces, such as parents, peers, school, and the media.

gender barriers: Culturally created barriers that exclude a particular gender (usually women) from full participation in society (e.g., employment).

gender identity/role: A cultural construct that gives us our social identity, status, and roles in society. We learn our gender identity and roles through enculturative forces, such as parents, peers, school, and media.

gender stratification: Usually refers to women who have unequal access to resources, opportunities, and prestige based on their gender. All known societies are patriarchal and therefore have some form of gender stratification, although in industrial countries, such as the United States, this form of stratification is disappearing.

global youth culture: A suggestion that youth around the world are slowly developing similar ideals, values, and customs, mainly due to global media.

globalization: A complex process that involves worldwide integration of economies, which has been assisted by global transportation and communication systems and information technology. Globalization has resulted in dramatic rises in inequalities, over-exploitation of the world's resources, and mass displacement of people.

117

glocalization: A combining of localization and globalization that refers to business interactions on a local, regional, and global scale. Goods produced have global markets, yet fulfill the needs of local consumers; for example, the modifications to Disney Tokyo to satisfy Japanese consumers.

graffiti: Images or lettering set on property not belonging to the artist. Considered vandalism by some, art by others. May be used as decoration or for socio-political commentary.

hegemony: Dominant nation imposing its vision of how citizens should live and think on another nation.

hip hop culture: A subcultural movement among youth who fancy a particular music style (rap and deejaying); visual art (graffiti and street art); fashion (baggy pants); and b-boy/b-girl(ing) (breakdancing, distinctive language, attitude, and popular lifestyle).

holistic approach/perspective: Anthropologists view the components or systems of a culture (economic, social, political, and religion) as an integrated whole, with each system influencing and being influenced by the other systems.

homogenization/homogenous: Becoming the same, or displaying similar characteristics, such as rock music overwhelming traditional ethnic music or modifying this music.

hybridization: In anthropology, the blending or mixing of cultural traits from more than one culture.

identity: Our sense of self and belonging, such as to a subcultural group like the Goths.

identity marker: Symbols or behaviours that give us our identity (e.g., clothing).

imagery: Visual or imaginative images drawn from the five senses that evoke memories.

indigenous peoples: Members of small-scale cultures who self-identify as the original inhabitants of the land based on a long history of occupation. Indigenous peoples the world over are threatened by state powers and economic development.

Internet: Worldwide network of interconnected computers that enables the almost instantaneous transmission of data from computer to computer.

marriage: The joining of two or more people to form conjugal bonds.

mass media: A form of communication that transmits images, ideas, and entertainment; includes television, radio, Internet, film, and literature, and may also include art.

microculture: Small groups with behaviour that separates them from mainstream culture (e.g., punks, skateboarders). Another word for subculture.

mock wedding: A reproduction of an actual wedding with no legal or moral significance. Often it is a parody of real weddings held on significant anniversaries.

modernity: The concept of being modern.

modernization: The process of making other societies over in the image of the West through changing their social, economic, political, and religious systems. Although officially designed to improve the quality of life of non-Westerners, this seldom happens; indeed, in most cases, modernization lowers the quality of life.

music: A form of artistic expression based on sounds and rhythms that are pleasing to the ear.

mythology: Stories perceived to be true by believers. Usually refer to religious accounts of the way things came to be the way they are.

national identity: Identifying with a particular country or nation.

nationalism: A sense of pride in one's nation.

naturalization: Absorbing and making one's own borrowed cultural elements.

netizens: People who regularly use the Internet and are comfortable doing so.

online ethnography: Ethnographic fieldwork conducted over the Internet.

participant observation: A research method whereby the anthropologist lives with the study group, learns their language, and develops a rapport with at least some members of the community who may also serve as key informants. The ethnographer closely observes the people as they go about their daily lives and, as much as possible, participates in their daily activities. Participant observation provides a first-hand descriptive account of the way people really live.

performance: Ritualized behaviour that is usually witnessed by other people (audience).

performance theory: Theoretical perspective that views human activities as experiences, values, and symbols that are presented, interpreted, and even transformed.

political resistance: Resistance to political domination.

popular culture: The culture of our everyday lives, such as television, sports, arts and crafts, fiction, and music.

protest songs: Songs that recount the struggles of a group and urge the struggle to continue (e.g., gangsta rap).

race: A misleading and inaccurate concept used to place individuals and populations into categories based on broad biological and/or behavioural traits.

racial barriers: Barriers in place to prevent members of a particular "race" from fully participating in and enjoying the benefits of society.

racial discrimination: Differential access to resources and opportunities based on racial categorization.

racial stereotyping: Attaching particular behaviours to a "race" based on little scientific data.

rap music: A distinctive style of music within hip hop culture that affords performers with a forum for cultural and political expression.

rite of intensification: A group ritual designed to deal with times of crisis.

119

rite of passage: Rituals that mark important stages in an individual's life (e.g., birth, puberty, marriage, and death).

ritual: An organized action to bring about expected results.

segregation: The separation of people based on ethnic, gender, racial, or age stereotyping.

socializing/socialization: Social interaction—visiting, talking, playing sports, etc.—between people.

solidarity/social solidarity: Group loyalty and cohesion. Members hold dear the same ideals and will defend those ideals and each other. Solidarity may be based on kinship, religious beliefs, occupation, etc.

status: Position within society.

stereotype/stereotyping: Entrenched ideas about other people that are not based on facts.

stratification: Placing people or groups into a hierarchy using various criteria. Those low on the hierarchy enjoy less access to resources and personal freedom.

subculture: Segments of a population that are distinct from mainstream culture, through ethnicity, class, religion, behaviour, and so on.

symbol: Objects, behaviours, places, and signs that conceptually represent ideas, beliefs, customs, and traditions. All languages are symbolic.

symbolism: The process of using symbols to represent abstract conditions.

tagging: Symbols or words that mark the graffiti writer's work and territory.

tattoos: Permanent marking of human skin, often for the purpose of marking identity.

television ethnography: The ethnographic study of television and its relationship to culture.

territoriality: A sense of ownership of a given region.

third places: A place where people gather that is outside the home or workplace.

virtual community: Social aggregates of people that conduct public discussions on subjects of mutual interest over the Internet.

QUESTIONS FOR CRITICAL CONSIDERATION

Chapter 1: What is Popular Culture?

1. Critics suggest that popular culture
    has become commercial culture
    and that most popular culture
    is too consumptive and exploit-
    ative. Provide examples of this
    commercialism and counter with
    examples that are not exploitative or
    consumer-driven.

2. Critically examine Fiske's statement
    that "popular culture is always part
    of power relations." Do you agree or
    disagree? Give examples to support
    your answer.

3. Identify ways that popular culture
    provides a window into other
    aspects of our cultural system—
    political, social, religious, and
    economic. What impact does popu-
    lar culture have on these systems?

4. The demise of popular culture may
    become a reality in some small-
    scale cultures. Investigate some of
    the strategies being employed to
    stem the tide of Western popular
    culture. In your opinion will these
    strategies work? Why or why not?

5. Further investigate the phenome-
    non of global youth culture. Do you
    think this demographic is going to
    create a homogenized global popu-
    lar culture? To answer this question,
    choose a form of popular culture
    (e.g., rap music) and examine its
    impact on youth around the world.

6. After you have read all the chapters
    in this book, return to this question:
    will we become a global village at
    the hands of popular culture? Based
    on the evidence and discussions in
    the following nine chapters, and
    your own personal experiences,
    answer this question.

7. Comment on the statement:
    "Today's pop counterculture,
    especially among the young, is
    an awesome mix of maximum
    mindlessness, minimum historical
    awareness, and a pathetic yearning
    for strawberry shortcake."

Chapter 2: The Study of Popular Culture

1. In *Pop Culture,* culture is very simply defined as "the whole way of life." Yet anthropologists define culture in myriad ways. Locate several other anthropological definitions of culture. Which definition seems most accurate to you? Why? Based on your research, attempt to create an inclusive definition of culture. Record the challenges you encounter in doing so.

2. In our global community, the boundaries between low and high culture appear to be blurring. Provide examples of this blurring.

3. Do you agree or disagree with the premise that all activities are performance? Based on your response, provide reasons and examples to back up your answer.

4. Choose a "performance" in your community and analyze the commentary (e.g., political, social, economic, religious) offered through this activity.

Chapter 3: Television

1. How would you respond to the statement: "Television rots our minds"?

2. Choose a popular television program and conduct an analysis of the societal values and norms it reflects. Is there a television program that has had an impact on you? In what way?

3. Do you think television influences the way you view the world? If yes, cite some example of how television programming has shaped or changed your way of thinking. If no, why not?

4. Recently there has been a great deal of controversy regarding the advertising of junk food, especially in light of the growing obesity problem among children. What are your thoughts on this movement? Do you believe advertising has any influence on food choices?

5. Choose a cultural group and conduct some research into their television programming. Is their programming influenced by North American television? Is this influence having an impact on their cultural practices and beliefs? Do they have local programming relevant to their lives that offsets foreign influences?

Chapter 4: Music

1. In your opinion, what is the most important role of popular music? How does it most affect or influence a culture? Cite examples.

2. Choose a popular music genre and trace its evolution. What alternative music genres, political movements, or historical events have affected popular culture?

3. Choose a popular music genre and analyze how it informs us about the subculture that most identifies with this genre.

4. Examine protest music in a given culture. Has this music effected any real change in society?

5. Censorship in music is an ongoing controversy. In your opinion, should lyrics or musical acts be controlled by censor ratings? Do some bands or other musical acts "cross the line"?

6. In your opinion, has hip hop culture and rap music aided in the quest for equality? Why or why not? Choose a specific hip hop culture to address this question.

Chapter 5: The Internet and Virtual Communities

1. Is the Internet a facilitator of cultural imperialism? To answer this question, choose one or two non-Western cultural groups or nations and research some form of popular culture (e.g., film). Examine whether Western popular culture is overriding local popular culture.

2. In what way do you think the Internet has most impacted on contemporary society? How is this influence likely to change in the near future?

3. Do you agree or disagree with the statement that the Internet increases social isolation?

4. Do you belong to a virtual community? If yes, in what ways does this virtual community fulfill your social needs?

5. Several studies of the value of virtual communities for elderly shut-ins have been conducted. Has any research been carried out on the influence of the Internet on children? What conclusions did this research reach?

6. Identify the most significant impact the Internet has had on human society, in your opinion. Explain your choice.

Chapter 6: Folk Art

1. In your opinion, is graffiti an art form? Why or why not?

2. What impact do you think the AIDS Memorial Quilt has had on the fight against HIV/AIDS?

3. In your extended family, are there any folk art traditions that have been handed down from generation to generation? What meaning and significance do these traditions hold in your family? In your opinion, has this folk art helped preserve your cultural traditions?

4. Compare and contrast folk art to popular art. Identify similarities and differences.

5. Choose a form of folk art and explore whether it has changed over time. What impact has outside forces (e.g., globalization) had on this folk art? Is the importance of this folk art diminishing?

6. Peteet's 1990 study of graffiti warfare brought to light some important roles of graffiti. Is this writing on the walls still continuing in 2008? Has the practice had any impact on the occupation of Palestine? Search for other nations where graffiti is used in social and political commentary and compare it to Palestinian graffiti.

Chapter 7: Body Art and Adornment

1. Tattooing is an expression of individuality and group identity. When you see someone with a tattoo or piercing, what message do they send to you? Do these messages differ depending on the type of body art or on the age, ethnicity, or gender of the wearer?

2. Since most people decorate, alter, or modify their bodies in some way, it is relevant to ask the question, why? Provide reasons for whatever body art or adornment you follow.

3. Anthropologist Margo Demello focused her ethnographic study on male convicts, although she did briefly mention that women also get tattoos. Conduct a research project into women's tattooing. What similarities and differences did you discover? Do tattoos create the same identity and sense of community in female populations?

4. Prison tattooing was identified as a tattooing community. Find other examples of subcultural tattooing communities. What characteristics do they share with the prison tattooing community? What characteristics are different, and why?

5. Do you have a tattoo? For what reason(s) did you join the tattooing community? If you do not have a tattoo, interview someone who does and identify their reasons for becoming tattooed.

Chapter 8: The Symbolic Meaning of Food

1. Food appears closely connected to holidays and festivals. Identify the festivities your family participates in and the way food factors into these celebrations.

2. Choose a celebratory meal—wedding feast, Thanksgiving dinner, Aboriginal pow wow, Ramadan iftar—and trace the origins and meaning of the food that is served.

3. Visit a local restaurant and observe the ambiance and the interaction between customers and between customers and staff. Is this restaurant fulfilling the mandate for a third place? Why or why not?

4. Dining out continues to be popular among people from virtually every socio-economic class; this is true in all urban areas around the world. How do rural people, especially in poor nations, fulfill this need to gather and socialize over food?

5. Traphagen and Brown clearly outline the research methods they used to collect their data while studying fast food in Japan. However, Reed-Danabay did not address her research methods while studying *la rôtie*. What research methods do you think she would have had to use to gather her ethnographic data?

6. Discuss and critique the statement: "Taste is a marker of class."

7. Identify new avenues of research into food as popular culture. Develop a plan (anthropological research design) for studying popular food behaviour in your community.

8. Have you ever participated in a Ukrainian Christmas Eve meal or a Hindu wedding feast? Find your own examples and address Tamara Kohn's statement that "cooking and eating are performances, rich with meaning" (2002: 2).

9. Compare and contrast the making of tamales with some shared cooking custom in your community (e.g., pie baking).

Chapter 9: Sports

1. Baseball crossed the "colour barrier" in 1946 amid a great deal of controversy. Was this the first sport to do so? Trace the removal of racial barriers in another sport. Was it as difficult as with baseball? What other barriers have sports erased? Are there still barriers to overcome?

2. Compare and contrast sports with religion. What similarities can you identify in the roles, purpose, and practices of sports and religion?

3. Sports have been accused of being an agent of cultural imperialism. Choose a cultural group other than the Dominican Republic and determine whether this is true in its case.

4. Identify the contributions sports make to society. Do these contributions stand alone or are they linked to other aspects of popular culture?

5. If you are a sports fan, analyze why you enjoy sports; if not, discuss why you do not enjoy sports.

6. Since sports are considered such a valuable commodity in contemporary societies, identity the main contributions of a sport to your community.

Chapter 10: Wedding Rituals

1. Why do you think wedding rituals evolved? What purpose(s) do they serve? Why have wedding rituals become so elaborate in many countries?

2. Identify the traditional wedding customs in your region/culture. How have they changed or hybridized over the years?

3. Wedding ceremonies affirm the joining of two people and two families. In your opinion, is this a necessary ritual in today's societies? Explain your reasoning.

4. Research the wedding rituals of a small-scale cultural group, and discuss the symbolism attached to these rituals.

5. Mock weddings are an extremely popular, albeit regional, custom that offers the community a social outlet to express the challenges of living and working on a prairie farm. Locate wedding customs in other cultures that may serve similar purposes.

SUGGESTED READINGS

Chapter 1: What is Popular Culture?

Browne, R.B., & Browne, P. (2001). *The guide to United States popular culture.* Bowling Green, OH: Bowling Green State University Popular Press.
Although ponderous in size and subject matter, and short on detail, this book is an encyclopedia of popular culture worthy of examination if for no other reason than it provides an extensive listing of popular culture that far exceeds the usual treatment of this topic.

Gans, H.J. (1974). *Popular culture and high culture. An analysis and evaluation of taste.* New York: Basic Books.
In this clearly written and fascinating book, Gans examines the politicization of culture. He critiques the critiquers of popular culture and succinctly examines the roles of popular culture versus high culture in North American society. Even though this work is dated, it still provides valuable insight into the tug of war between high and pop culture.

Martinez, D. (Ed.). *The world of Japanese popular culture: Gender, shifting boundaries and global cultures.* Cambridge: Cambridge University Press.
For a glimpse into popular culture outside the United States, this book provides a refreshing discussion of Japanese popular culture.

Chapter 2: The Study of Popular Culture

Bame, K.N. (1981). *Come to laugh: A study of African traditional theatre in Ghana.* Accra: Baatous Educational Enterprises.
An insightful look at Ghanaian concert parties as popular culture. The author's first-hand experiences with concert parties provide an added dimension to this brief introduction to a little known popular event.

Guss, David M. (2001). *The festive state. Race, ethnicity, and nationalism as cultural performance.* Berkeley, CA: University of California Press.
David Guss approaches the study of festivals from a performative perspective, where cultural concepts such as race, gender, nationhood, ethnicity, and history are contested in public displays.

128

Four case studies are used to make this point: Afro-Venezuelan celebrations in San Juan, the neo-Indian Day of the Monkey, the *mestizo* ritual of Tamunangue, and the British multinational tobacco corporation.

Szwed, J. (2005). *Crossovers: Essays on race, music, and American culture.* Philadelphia, PA: University of Pennsylvania Press.
In this comprehensive collection of 31 essays, commentaries, and reviews, a cornucopia of information on African-American and Afro-diasporic studies is cogently presented in a review of the intersections between music genres and culture, in particular race and artistic expressions. Many of the papers are on popular culture, including hip hop, the blues, and jazz in Africa, Russia, and Argentina.

Chapter 3: Television

Anger, D. (1999). *Other worlds. Society seen through soap opera.* Peterborough, ON: Broadview Press.
A refreshing ethnographic examination of the world of soap operas and the significance of this genre. Anthropologist Dorothy Anger demonstrates how soap operas shape perceptions and reflect current values and issues.

Casey, B., Casey, N., Calvert, B., French, L., & Lewis, J. (2002). *Television studies: The key concepts.* London: Routledge.
This comprehensive study of television addresses theoretical perspectives and looks at several popular genres, such as science fiction and soap operas.

Chalaby, J.K. (Ed.). (2005). *Transnational television worldwide: Towards a new media order.* London: I.B. Tauris.
A global perspective on the impact on other nations and cultures of media diffusion and globalization processes.

Ginsberg, F.D., Abu-Lughod, L., & Larkin, B. (Eds.). (2002). *Media worlds: Anthropology on new terrain* (pp. 115–33). Berkeley, CA: University of California Press.
In a much-needed revitalization of anthropology, this book presents a cross-cultural selection of ethnographies of media. The authors examine the role of various media around the world. Topics range from indigenous projects, the hidden agendas of state-controlled media, and the impact of media on local cultures.

Kottak, C.P. (1990). *Prime-time society: An anthropological analysis of television and culture.* Belmont, CA: Wadsworth Publishing Company.
Although there are many analyses of the impact of media, Kottak presents a comprehensive discussion of television's impact on culture from an anthropological perspective, including an examination of Brazil's *telenovelas.*

Chapter 4: Music

Brooker, W., & Jermyn, D. (Eds.). (2002). *The audience studies reader.* New York: Routledge.
A broad range of topics relevant to *Pop Culture* are considered in this book, including an essay on Beatlemania. Highly recommended.

Cushman, T. (1995). *Notes from the underground: Rock music counterculture in Russia.* Albany, NY: State University of New York Press.
An important ethnographic contribution to comparative popular culture literature that examines rock musicians and counterculture during the break-up of the Soviet Union. Cushman analyzes popular culture under state socialist conditions, the origins and perpetuation of counterculture, and its ultimate absorption into a capitalist economy.

Danielson, V., Marius, S., & Reynolds, D. (2002). *The Middle East. Garland Encyclopedia of world music, 6.* London: Routledge.
A composite of contemporary music cultures that not only discusses music but its relation to history, culture, and cultural influence from other groups. It also deals with popular music and the Western influence on other music.

129

Stokes, M. (1992). *The Arabesk debate: Music and musicians in modern Turkey.* Oxford: Oxford University Press.
An ethnographic study of *arabesk,* a popular music form in Istanbul that reflects the countercultural movements among disenfranchised urban Turks.

Waterman, C.A. (1990). *Juju: A social history and ethnography of an African popular music.* Chicago, IL: University of Chicago Press.
Waterman brings alive a unique type of African popular music as the Yoruba experience it. This is not only a history and ethnography of juju music but a discussion of its social significance.

Chapter 5: The Internet and Virtual Communities

Fishwich, M.W. (2004). *Probing popular culture: On and off the Internet.*
Philadelphia, PA: Haworth Press.
This book examines the impact of the Internet on our everyday lives and popular culture.

Ludlow, P., & Blankenship, L. (Eds.). (1996). *High noon on the electronic frontier: Conceptual issues in cyberspace.* Cambridge, MA: MIT Press.
A collection of essays written by scholars, aficionados of the Internet, and even hackers, discussing diverse topics such as censorship, community, hacking, and so on.

Rheingold, H. (2000). *The virtual community: Homesteading on the electronic frontier.* Cambridge, MA: MIT Press.
Howard Rheingold expounds on the Internet and cyberspace; many of his comments and vignettes are based on first-hand experience. He discusses the WELL (Whole Earth 'lectronic Link) virtual community, his first foray into cyberspace in the 1980s.

Chapter 6: Folk Art

Candida, F. (2001.) *Great masters of Mexican folk art.* New York: Harry N. Abrams.
An excellent source for information and illustration of Mexico's folk art tradition, this book emphasizes the continuity, vibrancy, and religious and social significance of folk art traditions.

Moeran, B. (1997). *Folk art potters of Japan: Beyond an anthropology of aesthetics.* Richmond, Surrey: Curzon Press.
In this ethnographic study of the Japanese folk art of *mingei* craft, Moeran considers some of the larger theoretical questions regarding aesthetics, Orientalism, and the world of art.

Phillips, S.A. (1999). *Wallbangin': Graffiti and gangs in L.A.* Chicago, IL: The University of Chicago Press.
Anthropologist Susan Phillips takes an in-depth, anthropological look at African-American and Chicano graffiti artists. She argues that graffiti is linked to political change, race relations, and aesthetic expression.

Chapter 7: Body Art and Adornment

Pitts, V.L. (2003). *In the flesh: The cultural politics of body modification.* New York: Palgrave MacMillan.
A fascinating examination of body modification subcultures and their political machinations.

Randall, H., & Polhemus, T. (1996). *The customized body.* London: Serpent's Tail.
This is an informative and visually stimulating examination of body art, including painting, tattooing, scarification, body piercing, make-up, and jewellery, as well as gender modification.

Thomas, N., Cole, A., & Douglas, B. (Eds.). (2005). *Tattoo: Bodies, art, and exchange in the Pacific and the West.* Durham, NC: Duke University Press.
A comprehensive examination of tattoos from an historical and ethnographic perspective.

Chapter 8: The Symbolic Meaning of Food

Counihan, C., & van Esterik, P. (Eds.). (1997). *Food and culture. A reader.* New York: Routledge.
A collection of essays on food, ranging from hunger and poverty, fasting and feasting, obesity, body image, anorexia nervosa, to food habits and the political economy of food.

Jacobs, M., & Scholliers, P. (Eds.). (2003). *Eating out in Europe: Picnics, gourmet dining, and snacks since the late eighteenth century.* New York: Berg.
This book examines the history and cultural change associated with eating out, including fast food in Britain, picnics in nineteenth-century France, snack shops in the Netherlands, canteens in Germany, and so on.

Lentz, C. (Ed.). (1999). *Changing food habits: Case studies from Africa, South America, and Europe.* Amsterdam: Harwood Academic Publishers.
An anthropological and historical account of the changing patterns of food consumption in Zambia, Ghana, Sudan, Germany, Switzerland, and the Ecuadorian Andes, paying particular attention to class, gender, and power relations.

Parkin, K.J. (2006). *Food is love: Food advertising and gender roles in modern America.* Philadelphia, PA: University of Pennsylvania Press.
This book is an insightful, scholarly examination of advertisers' exploitation of the traditional attitude that women, including American women, should express their love through food. Parkin discusses the perception that food preparation can be sexy, create marital bliss, and improve the status of the family— all if the right products are used.

Chapter 9: Sports

Blanchard, K. (1995). *The anthropology of sport: An introduction.* Rev. Ed. London: Bergin & Garvey.
In this volume, the cultural institution of sports is examined, including its history, theory, and practice.

Dyck, N. (2000). *Games, sports, and cultures.* New York: Berg.
This book provides a comprehensive examination of sports from an anthropological perspective. Of particular interest are discussions of indigenous sports.

Mandelbaum, M. (2004). *The meaning of sports: Why Americans watch baseball, football, and basketball and what they see when they do.* New York: PublicAffairs.
This comprehensive book answers many of the questions readers may have regarding the significance of sports in our everyday life.

Mochizuki, K. (1993). *Baseball saved us.* New York: Lee & Low Books.
This is the story of a young boy of Japanese descent who is imprisoned along with his parents in an Idaho internment camp during World War II. His father decides to build a baseball diamond, partly for something to do, but mostly to give his fellow prisoners a renewed sense of dignity and control over their lives. Although this is a children's book, the underlying message of the harm that prejudice, ignorance, and fear can cause is significant to readers of all ages, and the role baseball played in giving Shorty a way of dealing with his life highlights one of the values of sports.

Chapter 10: Wedding Rituals

Foster, H.B., & Johnson, D.C. (Eds.). (2003). *Wedding dresses across cultures.* New York: Berg.
A collection of essays discussing wedding traditions and the ritual function of wedding attire in Asia, Africa, Europe, and North America.

Wardle, L.D. (Ed.). (2003). *Marriage and same-sex unions: A debate.* Westport, CT: Praeger.
An in-depth collection of articles on same-sex marriages that range from the legal to religious perspective and include such topics as gender, equality, and the history of the gay rights struggle.

REFERENCES

Aaron, H. (1999, June 14). Jackie Robinson. *The Time 100*. Retrieved 29 April 2007 from http://www.time.com/time/time100/heroes/profile/robinson03.html.

Abu-Lughod, L. (1997). The interpretation of culture(s) after television. Special issue: The fate of "culture": Geertz & beyond. *Representatives* 59: 109–34.

Abu-Lughod, L. (2002a). Egyptian melodrama—technology of the modern subject? In F.D. Ginsberg, L. Abu-Lughod, & B. Larkin (Eds.), *Media worlds: Anthropology on new terrain* (pp. 115–33). Berkeley, CA: University of California Press.

Abu-Lughod, L. (2002b). The objects of soap opera: Egyptian television and the cultural politics of modernity. In S. Schech & J. Haggis (Eds.), *Development: A cultural studies reader* (pp. 311–23). Oxford: Blackwell Publishing.

Al-Mazeedi, M.L., & Ibrahim, A.I. (1998). The education and social effects of the Internet on Kuwait University students. Paper presented to the Conference on Information Superhighway, Safat, Kuwait.

Alward, M.M. (1999). *The old-fashioned way: Mock wedding*. Retrieved 27 January 2006 from http://www.happy-anniversary.com/anniversaries_celebrated/10/old_fashion_mock_wedding.html.

America Plus. (2006, December 1). *Eye on Brazil*. Orbit Television, Cairo Egypt.

Anderson, B. (1991). *Imagined communities: Reflections on the origin and spread of nationalism*. Rev. ed. New York: Verso.

Anger, D. (1999). *Other worlds. Society seen through soap opera*. Peterborough, ON: Broadview Press.

Appadurai, A. (1986). Theory in anthropology: Center and periphery. *Comparative Studies in Society and History* 28(2): 356–61.

Appadurai, A. (1990). Disjuncture and difference in the global economy. In M. Featherstone (Ed.), *Global culture: Nationalism, globalization and modernity* (pp. 295–310). London: Sage.

Armbrust, W. (1996). *Mass culture and modernism in Egypt.* Cambridge: University of Cambridge Press.

Armstrong, G., & Guilianotti, R. (Eds.). (1997). *Entering the field: New perspectives on world football.* Oxford: Berg.

134 Armstrong, G., & Giulianotti, R. (1999). *Football cultures and identities.* Houndsmills, UK: MacMillan Press.

Asad, T. (1993). *Genealogies of religion: Disciplines and reasons of power in Christianity and Islam.* Baltimore, MD: Johns Hopkins University Press.

Aufderheide, P. (1993). Latin American grassroots video. Beyond television. *Public Culture.* Chicago.

Austin, J. (2002). Review of *Wallbangin': Graffiti and gangs in L.A. American Ethnologist* 29(2): 450–51.

Baca, J. (1995). Whose monument where? Public art in a many-culture society. In S. Lacy (Ed.), *Mapping the terrain, new genre public art* (pp. 131–38). Seattle, WA: Bay Press.

Back, L., Crabbe, T., & Solomos, J. (2001). *The changing face of football: Racism, identity, and multiculture in the English game.* Oxford: Berg.

Bame, K.N. (1981). *Come to laugh: A study of African traditional theatre in Ghana.* Accra: Baatous Educational Enterprises.

Bankes, J. (1991). *The Pittsburgh Crawfords.* Dubuque, IA: William C. Brown.

Baxter, T. (2006). An art lesson in Rio. *CNN.com.* Retrieved 4 December 2006 from http://www.cnn.com/2006/WORLD/americas/11/30/baxter.rio/index.html.

Beeman, W. (1993). The anthropology of theatre and spectacle. *Annual Review of Anthropology* 22: 369–93.

Beeman, W.O. (1997). *Performance theory in an anthropology program.* Retrieved 23 October 2007 from http://www.brown.edu/Departments/Anthropology/publications/PerformanceTheory.htm.

Best, E. (1934). The Maori as he was: A brief account of life as it was in pre-European days. New Zealand Electronic Text Centre. Retrieved 6 May 2007 from http://www.nzetc.org/tm/scholarly/tei-BesMaor-c6-2-1.html.

Best, S., & Kellner, D. (1999). Rap, Black rage, and racial difference. *Enculturation* 2(2): n.p. Retrieved 27 June 2007 from http://enculturation.gmn.edu/2_2/best-kellner.html.

Blanchard, K. (1995). *The anthropology of sport.* Westport, CT: Bergin & Garvey.

Block, M. (2000). Here comes a regular. *My words worth*. Retrieved 29 May 2007 from http://marylaine.com/myword/3rdplace.html

Bohannan, P. (1991). *We the alien: An introduction to cultural anthropology*. Long Grove, IL: Waveland Press.

Bourdieu, P. (1984). *Distinction. A social critique of the judgement of taste*. Richard Nice, trans. Cambridge, MA: Harvard University Press.

Bowen, T.E. (1999). Graffiti art: A contemporary study of Toronto artists. *Studies of Art Education. A Journal of Issues and Research* 41(1): 23–39.

Boyd, S. (2004). Being wired encourages human contact. *The third space*. Retrieved 29 May 2007 from http://www.corante.com/getreal/archives/004843.html.

Breslin, M.M. (2006, October 29). The family that tattoos together...: More parents are welcoming teens' body art—and taking part. *Chicago Tribune*. Retrieved 17 May 2007 from http://infotrac-college.thomsonlearning.com/itw/infomark/807/258/6241896w18/purl=rci_WAD_0_A153485822&dyn=3!ar_fmt?sw_aep=olr_wad.

Browne, R.B., & Browne, P. (2001). Introduction. In R.B. Browne & P. Browne (Eds.), *The guide to United States popular culture* (pp. 1–4). Bowling Green, OH: Bowling Green State University Popular Press.

Brownell, E. (1999). Why study sports in China? In N. Dyck (Ed.), *Games, sports and cultures*. New York: Berg.

Browning, B. (1995). *Samba: Resistance in motion*. Bloomington, IN: Indiana University Press.

Bulag, U.E. (2003). Review of *Mongolian music, dance, and oral narrative: Performing diverse identities*. *American Anthropologist* 105(2): 452–53.

Caglar, A.S. (1999). Fast food and ethnic business: The story of *doner kabab* in Berlin. In C. Lentz (Ed.), *Changing food habits: Case studies from Africa, South America, and Europe*. Amsterdam: Harwood Academic Publishers.

Calhoun, D.B. (1987). *Sport, culture and personality*. Campaign, IL: Human Kinetics.

CBC News. (2007). *Backyard barbecuing. The quest for fire*. Retrieved 17 November 2007 from http://www.cbc.ca/news/background/bbq/.

CBC News Broadcast. (2006, February 10). President of International Olympic Committee.

Chayko, M. (2003, November). Review of *The internet in everyday life*. *Contemporary Sociology* 32(6): 728–30.

135

Chen, W., Boase, J., & Wellman, B. (n.d.). *The global villagers: Comparing internet users and uses around the world*. Retrieved 21 November 2006 from http://www.chass.utoronto.ca/~wellman/publications/villagers/gddi3-.

Christiansen, N.B. (2003). *Inuit in cyberspace. Embedding offline identities online*. Copenhagen: Museum Tusculanum Fortlag.

Clark, L. (1998). Dating on the Net: Teens and the rise of "pure" relationships. In S. Jones (Ed.), *Cybersociety: Revisiting computer-mediated communication and community* (pp. 159–83). Thousand Oaks, CA: Sage Publications.

Clark, W. (1993). Review of *Pop art and consumer culture: American supermarket. The Journal of American History* 79(4): 1682–83.

Collins, J. (1976). Comic opera in Ghana. *African Arts* 9(2): 50–57.

Collins, J. (1994). The Ghanaian concert party: African popular entertainment at the cross roads. Ph.D. thesis. State University of New York at Buffalo.

Combs, J. (1984). *Polpop: Politics and popular culture in America*. Bowling Green, OH: Bowling Green State University Popular Press.

Conway-Long, D. (1998, September). Review of *Entering the field: New perspectives on world football. American Anthropology* 100(3): n.p.

Correll, S. (1995). The ethnography of an electronic bar. The lesbian café. *Journal of Contemporary Ethnography* 24(3): 270–98.

Counihan, C.M. (1999). *The anthropology of food and body: Gender, meaning, and power*. London: Routledge.

Counts, D.A., & Counts, D.R. (1996). *Over the next hill. An ethnography of RVing seniors in North America*. Peterborough, ON: Broadview Press.

Cushman, T. (1995). *Notes from the underground: Rock music counterculture in Russia*. Albany, NY: State University of New York Press.

D'Acci, J. (2004). Television, representation, and gender. In R.C. Allen & A. Hill (Eds.), *The television studies reader* (pp. 373–88). New York: Routledge.

Davis, J. (1977). *People of the Mediterranean. An essay in comparative social anthropology*. London: Routledge and Kegan Paul.

Davis, N.Z. (1975). The reasons for misrule. In *Society and culture in modern France* (pp. 97–123). Stanford, CA: Stanford University Press.

Demello, M. (1993). The convict body. Tattooing among male American prisoners. *Anthropology Today* 9(6): 10–13.

Digit. (2006, November 29). *Viva design*. Retrieved 1 December 2006 from http://www.digitmag.co.uk/features/index.cfm?FeatureID=1536.

Dompere, K.K., & Fadopé, C.M. (1997). African immigrant music and dance in Washington, D.C. *Articles from the 1997 Festival of American Folklife Program Book*. Retrieved 7 July 2007 from http://www.folklife.si.edu/resources/Festival1997/musicand.htm.

Dove, L. (n.d.). *The history of barbecue in the South*. Retrieved 4 August 2007 from http://xroads.virginia.edu/~CLASS/MA95/dove/history.htm.

Duany, J. (1984). Popular music in Puerto Rico: Toward an anthropology of salsa. *Latin American Music Review* 5(2): 186–216.

Duke, V., & Crolley, L. (1996). *Football, nationality, and the state*. Essex, UK: Longman.

Dunlap, H. (1951). Games, sports, dancing, and other vigorous recreational activities and their function in Samoan culture. *Research Quarterly* 22: 298–311.

Durán, J. (2002). Nation and translation: The "Pachuco" in Mexican popular culture: Germán Valdéz's Tin Tan. *The Journal of the Midwest Modern Language Association* 34(2): 41–40.

Dyck, N., & Archest, E.P. (2003). *Sport, dance, and embodied identities*. New York: Berg.

Earthwatch. (n.d.). *Net of the north. Canada's Inuit people get a tool to help forge their new land*. Retrieved 30 October 2006 from : http://www.cyber24.com/nun1/5_129.nun.

Edwards, W. (1989). *Modern Japan through its weddings: Gender, person, and society in ritual portrayal*. Stanford, CA: Stanford University Press.

Epstein, D. (2001). *20th century pop culture. The 90s*. Philadelphia: Chelsea House Publishers.

Erickson, J. (1999). Performing distinctions. *A Journal of Performance and Art:* 98–104.

Etylin, V. (2007). *Russia's reindeer herder peoples*. Retrieved 6 May 2007 from http://www.ip-ipy.org/filarkiv/File/presntations/ealat_kautokeino2007/Vladimir_Etylin.pdf.

Fabian, J. (1978). Popular culture in Africa: Findings and conjectures. *Africa* 48(4): 315–34.

Fabian, J. (1990). *Power and performance*. Madison, WI: Routledge.

137

Fedorak, S. (2006). *Windows on the world. Case studies in anthropology.* Toronto: Nelson Thomson Learning.

Fernandes, S. (2003). Fear of a black nation: Local rappers, transnational crossings, and state power in contemporary Cuba. *Anthropological Quarterly* 76(4): 575–608.

Fernandez, A. (2000). ¿Paesia urbana? o la nueva trova de los noventa. *El caiman barbudo* 296: 4–14.

Fernandez, A. (2002). SBS. ¿Timba con rap? El hip hop de la pótemica. *Revista salsa Cubana* 5(17): 43–45.

Fisher, M.F.K. (1942). *How to cook a wolf.* New York: Duell, Sloan & Pierce.

Fiske, J. (1989). *Understanding popular culture.* London: Routledge.

Fiske, J. (2003). Understanding popular culture. In W. Brooker & D. Jermyn (Eds.), *The audience studies reader* (pp. 112–16). London: Routledge.

Fordham, P. (2007, May 5). *Jesse Bell "Sis" Telfair.* Retrieved 11 May 2007 from http://www.oxford9.com/jessie_bell_telfair.htm.

Franklin, I. (2001). Abstract for *Inside out: Postcolonial subjectivities and everyday life online.* In *International Feminist Journal of Politics* 3(3): 387–422. Retrieved 30 October 2006 from http://www.ingentaconnect.com/content/routledg/rfjp/2001/00000003/00000003/art00004.

Freccero, C. (1999). *Popular culture: An introduction.* New York: New York University Press.

Frith, S. (1992). The cultural study of popular music. In L. Grossberg, C. Nelson, & P. Treichler (Eds.), *Cultural Studies* (pp. 74–86). New York: Routledge.

Futrell, J. (1998). Enterprise zones. *Waitrose Food Illustrated.* Retrieved 29 May 2007 from http://www.waitrose.com/food_drink/wfi/foodaroundtheworld/theamericas/9808060.asp.

Gans, H.J. (1974). *Popular culture and high culture. An analysis and evaluation of taste.* New York: Basic Books.

Gell, A. (1993). *Wrapping in images: Tattooing in Polynesia.* Oxford: Clarendon Press.

Ghirardini, J. (2001, December 31). Old-fashioned gathering places breathe new life into Atlanta-area towns. *Atlanta Journal-Constitution.* Retrieved 1 June 2007 from http://infotrac-college.thomsonlearning.com/itw/infomark/299/522/2752265w16/purl=rci_WAD_0_CJ120657663&dyn=4!ar_fmt?sw_aep=olr_wad.

Gianis, R. (2006, February). Face vessels: Original African-American folk art. *Arts & Activities* 139(i): 18. Retrieved 9 May 2007 from http://infotrac-college. thomsonlearning.com/itw/ infomark/880/320/1145362w17/ purl=rci_WAD_0_A141447009& dyn=19!ar_fmt?sw_aep=olr_wad.

Gilbert, M. (1998). Concert parties: Paintings and performance. *Journal of Religion in Africa* 28(1): 62–92.

Gilbert, M. (2000). *Hollywood icons, local demons: Ghanaian popular paintings by Mark Anthony.* Hartford, CT: Trinity College.

Gillespie, M. (2003). Television, ethnicity and cultural change. In W. Brooker & D. Jermyn (Eds.), *The audience studies reader* (pp. 315–321). London: Routledge.

Gilroy, P. (1987). *There ain't no black in the Union Jack.* London: Routledge.

Ginsberg, F. (1994). Culture/media: A (mild) polemic. *Anthropology Today* 19(2): 5–15.

Ginsberg, F., Abu-Lughod, L., & Larkin, B. (Eds.). (2002). Introduction. *Media worlds: Anthropology on new terrain* (pp. 1–36). Berkeley, CA: University of California Press.

Giroux, H. (1992). Resisting difference: Cultural studies and the discourse of critical pedagogy. L. Grossberg, C. Nelson & P. Treichler (Eds.), *Cultural Studies.* New York: Routledge.

Goffman, G. (1959). *The presentation of self in everyday life.* Garden City, NJ: Doubleday.

Good Morning America. (2006, November 15). *Seven wonders of the world* segment.

Gottlieb, A. (1997). The perils of popularizing anthropology. *Anthropology Today* 13(1): 1–2.

Handwerk, B. (2002, October 11). Tattoos—From taboo to mainstream. *National Geographic News.* Retrieved 15 May 2007 from http://news.nationalgeographic. com/news/2002/10/1011_021011_ taboo.html.

Hansen, K.T. (1999). The cook, his wife, the madam and their dinner: Cooking, gender and class in Zambia. C. Lentz (Ed.), *Changing food habits: Case studies from Africa, South America and Europe* (pp. 73–90). New York: Routledge.

139

Hathaway, N. (2007, April). Graffiti and guerrilla art. *Arts & Activities* 141(3): 38. Retrieved 10 May 2007 from http://infotrac-college.thomsonlearning.com/itw/infomark/519/532/5584915w19/purl=rc1_WAD_0_A161011367&dyn=14!xrn_52_0_A161011367?sw_aep=olr_wad.

Heaven, C., & Tubridy, M. (2002b). Global youth culture and youth identity. *UNESCO* (pp. 149–160). Retrieved 13 June 2007 from http://www.google.ca/search?hl=en&ned=&q=Global+youth+culture+and+youth+identity&btnmeta%3Dsearch%3Dsearch=Search+the+Web.

Hoffman, E. (2001). Quilts. In R.B. Browne & P. Browne (Eds.), *The guide to United States popular culture* (p. 654). Bowling Green, OH: Bowling Green State University Popular Press.

Hoover, M. (2001). Coffeehouses. In R.B. Browne & P. Browne (Eds.), *The guide to United States popular culture* (pp. 184–85). Bowling Green, OH: Bowling Green State University Popular Press.

Horkheimer, M., & Adorno, T. (1992). *Dialectic of enlightenment.* New York: Herder and Herder.

Howard, P.E.N., Rainie, L., & Jones, S. (2002). Days and nights on the internet. In B. Wellman & C. Haythornthwaite (Eds.), *The internet in everyday life* (pp. 45–73). Oxford: Blackwell Publishing.

Hunt, A. (1999). When did the sixties happen? Searching in new directions. *Journal of Social History* 33(1): 147.

Hunter, L. (n.d.). Popular culture. *Globalization and Autonomy Online Compendium.* UBC Press. Retrieved 26 June 2007 from http://anscombe.mcmaster.ca/globa11/glossary_entry.jsp?id=C0.0008.

Internet World Stats. (2006). *Internet usage statistics—The big picture.* Retrieved 28 September 2006 from http://www.internetworldstats.com/stats.htm.

Jackson, K.M. (2001). Sesame Street. In R.B. Browne & P. Browne (Eds.), *The guide to United States popular culture* (pp. 726–27). Bowling Green, OH: Bowling Green State University Popular Press.

Jackson-Doling, A. (2000). Introduction. In T.C. Choi & M. Isaak (Eds.), *The food of Vietnam: Authentic recipes from the heart of Indochina.* Boston, MA: Periplus Editions (HK) Ltd.

Jefkin, D. (2004, January-February). Tribal identity through body art. *Skipping Stones* 16(1): 34. Retrieved 27 May 2007 from http://infotrac-college.thomsonlearning.com/itw/infomark/166/13/1743305w16/purl=rc1_WAD_0_A113052115&dyn=23!ar_fmt?sw_aep=olr_wad.

140

Jensen, R. (2001). The internet. In R.B. Browne & P. Browne (Eds.), *The guide to United States popular culture* (pp. 430–31). Bowling Green, OH: Bowling Green State University Popular Press.

Jones, A. (1998). *Body art/performing the subject.* Minneapolis, MN: University of Minnesota Press.

Kanayama, T. (2000). *The pilot study of the uses of electronic mail by the elderly.* Paper presented at the 2000 Mid-Year Conference of AEJMC Graduate Education Interest Group, Boulder, CO. 14–16 April.

Kellner, D. (1995). *Media culture: Cultural studies, identity, and politics between the modern and the postmodern.* New York: Routledge.

Kidd, D. (2007). Harry Potter and the functions of popular culture. *The Journal of Popular Culture* 40(1): 69–89.

Kim, S. (1998). Cultural imperialism on the internet. *The Edge: The E-Journal of Intercultural Relations* 1(4).

Klein, A.M. (1995). Culture, politics, and baseball in the Dominican Republic. *Latin American Perspectives* 22(3): 111–30.

Kohn, T. (2002). Mom's pecan rolls. *Anthropology Today* 18(2): 20–21.

Kondo, D. (1997). *About face: Performing race on fashion and theatre.* London: Routledge.

Kononenko, N. (1998). *Traditional Ukrainian wedding rituals.* Retrieved 28 January 2006 from http://www.brama.com/art/wedding.html.

Kosut, M. (2006). An ironic fad: The commodification and consumption of tattoos. *The Journal of Popular Culture* 39(6): 1035–48.

Kottak, C.P. (1990). *Prime-time society. An anthropology analysis of television and culture.* Belmont, CA: Wadsworth Publishing Co.

Krutak, L. (1997). *The Arctic.* Tattooed Singles.com. Retrieved 16 May 2007 from http://tattoos.com/ARCTIC.htm.

Krutak, L. (2005). Four tattoo artists in Havana. *Piercing and penetration in the Arctic.* Retrieved 15 May 2007 from http://www.vanishingtattoo.com/artic_piercing.htm.

Krutak, L. (2006a). At the tail of the dragon: The vanishing tattoos of the Li people. *Piercing and penetration in the Arctic.* Retrieved 15 May 2007 from http://www.vanishingtattoo.com/artic_piercing.htm.

Krutak, L. (2006b). Piercing and penetration: Body arts of the Unangan, Alutiiq, and Chugach of Alaska. *Piercing and penetration in the Arctic.* Retrieved 15 May 2007 from http://www.vanishingtattoo.com/artic_piercing.htm.

141

Kup, K. (1956). Asian artists in crystal. *The Metropolitan Museum of Art Bulletin,* New Series 14(7): 174–80.

Lamberth, S. (n.d.). The anthropology of performance. *Subdisciplines: Anthropology of performance.* Retrieved 23 October 2007 from http://www.indiana.edu/~anthro/theory_pages/performance.htm.

Lashua, B. (2006). The arts of the remix: Ethnography and rap. *Anthropology Matters Journal* 8(2). Retrieved 30 May 2007 from http://www.anthropologymatters.com/journal/2006–2/lashua_2006_the.htm.

Lee, J.H. (n.d.). *Hmong quilts—pa ndau—reflect Hmong history.* Associated Press. Retrieved 13 May 2007 from http://www.hmongnet.org/culture/pandau2.html.

Lentz, C. (Ed.). (1999). *Changing food habits: Case studies from Africa, South America, and Europe.* Amsterdam: Harwood Academic Publishers.

Levine, L.W. (1988). *Highbrow/lowbrow: The emergence of cultural hierarchy in America.* Cambridge, MA: Harvard University Press.

Lewis, L.G. (1978). *The Book of Dede Korkut.* New York: Praeger Publishers, Inc.

Ley, D., & Cybriwsky, R. (1974). Urban graffiti as territorial markers. *Annals of the Association of American Geographers* 64(4): 491–505.

Lien, M.E. (2002). Review of *Changing food habits: Case studies from Africa, South America and Europe. American Ethnologist* 29(4): 1037–38.

Lineberry, C. (2007). Tattoos. The ancient and mysterious history. *Smithsonian.com.* Retrieved 11 March 2007 from http://www.smithsonianmagazine.com/issues/2007/january/tattoo.php.

Lockard, C.A. (2001). Calypso. In R.B. Browne & P. Browne (Eds.), *The guide to United States popular culture* (pp. 133–34). Bowling Green, OH: Bowling Green State University Popular Press.

Lysloff, R.T.A. (2005). Musical community on the internet: An online ethnography. *Cultural Anthropology* 18(3): 233–63.

Magoulick, M. (n.d.). *Fieldwork/ethnography and performance theory.* Retrieved 23 October 2007 from http://www.faculty.de.gcsu.edu/~mmagouli/performance.htm.

Mahon, M. (2004). *Right to rock: The Black Rock Coalition and the cultural politics of race.* Durham, NC: Duke University Press.

Malaquais, D. (2001). Hollywood icons, local demons. *American Anthropologist* 102(4): 870–82.

142

Mandelbaum, M. (2004). *The meaning of sports. Why Americans watch baseball, football, and basketball and what they see when they do.* New York: Public Affairs.

McGee, C. (1998). Yarn paintings: Huichol myths and stories. *Planeta. com. Global Journal of Practical Ecotourism.* Retrieved 13 May 2007 from http://www.planeta.com/planeta/98/1198yarn.html.

McKinley, J. (2007, January 31). Fight over quilt reflects changing times in battle against AIDS. *The New York Times*, A16. Retrieved 9 May 2007 from http://infotrac-college.thomsonlearning.com/itw/infomark/880/320/1145362w17/purl=rc1_WAD_0_A158607659&dyn=25!ar_fmt?sw_aep=olr_wad.

Meadows, M. (1996). Indigenous cultural diversity: Television Northern Canada. *Culture and policy* 7: 25–44.

Meek, J. (2004). *Get a life.* Retrieved 27 January 2007 from http://www.guardian.co.uk/g2/story/0,1274712,00.html.

Miller, D. (1995). Consumption and commodities. *Annual Review of Anthropology* 24: 141–61.

Miller, D. (1998). *A theory of shopping.* Ithaca, NY: Cornell University Press.

Miller, D. (2001). *Car cultures.* Oxford: Berg.

Miller, L. (1995). Women and children first: Gender and the settling of the electronic frontier. In J. Brook and I. Boal (Eds.), *Resisting the virtual life* (pp. 49–58). San Francisco, CA: City Lights.

Mintz, S.W. (1985). *Sweetness and power: The place of sugar in modern history.* New York: Viking.

Mintz, S.W., & Du Bois, C.M. (2002). The anthropology of food and eating. *Annual Review of Anthropology* 31: 99–119.

Mitgang, H. (1989, July 15). Book of the times; Japanese put a spin on baseball. *The New York Times.* Retrieved 6 May 2007 from http://query.nytimes.com/gst/fullpage.html?res=950DE5D91731F936A25754C0A96F948260.

Moeran, B. (1997). *Folk art potters in Japan. Beyond an anthropology of aesthetics.* Richmond, UK: Curzon Press.

Nagelberg, K.M. (2001). Sainte-Marie, Buffy. In R.B. Browne & P. Browne (Eds.), *The guide to United States popular culture* (p. 705). Bowling Green, OH: Bowling Green State University Popular Press.

National Geographic Society. (2006). *Tuva Artists.* World Music. Retrieved 7 June 2007 from http://worldmusic.nationalgeographic.com/worldmusic/view/page.basic/country/content.country/tuva_828.

143

Newcomb, H., & Hirsch, P.M. (2000). Television as a cultural forum. In H. Newcomb (Ed.), *Television: The critical view,* 6th ed. (pp. 561–73). New York: Oxford University Press.

Nie, N.H., & Erbring, L. (2000). *Internet and society: A preliminary report.* Retrieved 19 November 2006 from http://www.stanford.edu/group/siqss/.

Noverr, D.A. (2001). Sports and popular literature. In R.B. Browne & P. Browne (Eds.), *The guide to United States popular culture* (pp. 767–69). Bowling Green, OH: Bowling Green State University Popular Press.

Ohnuki-Tierney, E. (1997). McDonald's in Japan: Changing manners and etiquette. In J.L. Watson (Ed.), *Golden Arches East: McDonald's in East Asia* (pp. 161–82). Stanford, CA: Stanford University Press.

Oldenburg, R. (1999). *The great good place: Cafés, coffee shops, bookstores, bars, hair salons, and other hangouts at the heart of a community.* New York: Marlowe & Co.

Ortner, S.B. (1995). Resistance and the problem of ethnographic refusal. *Comparative studies in society and history* 37(1): 173–93.

Ortner, S.B. (1998). Generation X: Anthropology in a media-saturated world. *Cultural Anthropology* 13(3): 414–40.

Otnes, C.C., & Pleck, E.H. (2003). *Cinderella dreams: the allure of the lavish wedding.* Berkeley, CA: University of California Press.

Ottenheimer, H.J. (2006). Crossing, creolization, and the African roots of American culture. *American Anthropologist* 108(3): 528–30.

Parkinson, R. (2007). Top 10 Symbolic Chinese Foods: From Fish to Fowl. *Aboutdot.com: Chinese Cuisine.* Retrieved 5 August 2007 from http://chinesefood.about.com/od/foodfestivals/tp/foodsymbolism.htm.

Peace, W.J. (2000). Review of Body art: Marks of identity, *American Museum of Natural History, American Anthropologist* 102(3): 589–93.

Pegg, C. (2001). *Mongolian music, dance, and oral narrative: Performing diverse identities.* Seattle, WA: University of Washington Press.

Peteet, J. (1996). The writing on the walls: The graffiti of the Intefada. *Cultural Anthropology* 11(2): 139–59.

Peters, B. (2003). Qu(e)erying comic book culture and representations of sexuality in Wonder Woman. CLC Web: Comparative Literature and Culture 5(3):6 Retrieved 19 February 2009 from http://docs.lib.purdue.edu/clcweb/vol5/iss3/6.

Peterson, D.R. (2001). Square dancing. In R.B. Browne & P. Browne (Eds.), *The guide to United States popular culture* (pp. 780–81). Bowling Green, OH: Bowling Green State University Popular Press.

Phillips, S. (1999). *Graffiti and gangs in L.A.* Chicago, IL: University of Chicago Press.

Polhemus, T., & Randall, H. (2000). *The customized body.* London and New York: Serpent's Tail.

Polish Art Center. (n.d.). *Polish paper cuts (wycinanki).* Retrieved 12 June 2007 from http://polartcenter.com/Wycinanki_Paper_Cuts_s/169.htm.

Pottier, J. (1999). *Anthropology of food: The social dynamics of food security.* Malden, MA: Blackwell.

Potuoğlu-Cook, O. (2006). Sweat, power, and art: Situating belly dancers and musicians in contemporary Istanbul. *Journal of Musical Anthropology of the Mediterranean* 11. Retrieved 13 March 2007 from http://www.levi.provincia.venezia.it/ma/index/number11/potuoglu/pot_0.htm.

Powers, L.A. (2001). Break Dancing. In R.B. Browne & P. Browne (Eds.), *The guide to United States popular culture* (pp. 114–15). Bowling Green, OH: Bowling Green State University Popular Press.

Pulliam, J.M. (2001). *All my children.* In R.B. Browne & P. Browne (Eds.), *The guide to United States popular culture* (pp. 24–25). Bowling Green, OH: Bowling Green State University Popular Press.

Reed-Danabay, D. (1996). Champagne and chocolate. "Taste" and inversion in a French wedding ritual. *American Anthropologist* 98(4): 750–61.

Rheingold, H. (1993). *The virtual community: Homesteading on the electronic frontier.* Reading, MA: Addison-Wesley Pub. Co.

Rheingold, H. (1995). *The Virtual community—Surfing the internet.* London: Minerva.

Richards, M., & French, D. (2000). Globalisation, television, and Asia. In D. French & M. Richards (Eds.), *Television in contemporary Asia* (pp. 13–28). Thousand Oaks, CA: Sage.

Rogosin, D. (1985). *Invisible men: Life in baseball's Negro League.* New York: Atheneum.

Rose, T. (1994). *Black noise: rap music and black culture in contemporary America.* Hanover, NH: Wesleyan University Press.

145

Rosendorf, N.M. (2000). Social and cultural globalization: Concepts, history, and America's role. In J.S. Nye & J.D. Donahue (Eds.), *Governances in a globalizing world* (pp. 109–34). Washington, DC: Brookings Institution Press.

Rosenhouse, J. (2003). *A comparative study of women's wedding songs in colloquial Arabic.* Retrieved 4 June 2007 from http://www.orinst.ox.ac.uk/nme/nesp/middle.htm.

Ross, A. (1989). *No respect: Intellectuals and popular culture.* New York: Routledge.

Royce, A.P. (2001). Dancing the nation. *American Anthropologist* 103(2): 539–41.

RussianLegacy.com. (2003). *Russian nesting dolls.* Retrieved 13 May 2007 from http://www.russianlegacy.com/nestingdolls.htm#history.

Sadler, S. (2004). *Easter eggs, Easter bunnies, and Christian tradition.* Retrieved 6 December 2006 from http://www.du.edu/~ssadler/Easter.html.

Sanders, C.R. (2001). Tattoos. In R.B. Browne & P. Browne (Eds.), *The guide to United States popular culture* (pp. 806–07). Bowling Green, OH: Bowling Green State University Popular Press.

Sands, B. (1999). *Anthropology, sport, and culture.* Westport, CT: Bergin & Garvey.

Schildkrout, E. (2001). Body art as visual language. *Anthro Notes:* 1–8.

Scott, K. (1998). *Girls need modems: Cyberculture and women's ezines.* Master's research paper, York University, Toronto. Retrieved 29 October 2006 from http://www.stumptuous.com/mrp.html.

Shuman, M.K. (1991). Maya popular culture. In R.B. Browne & P. Browne (Eds), *Digging into popular culture: Theories and methodologies in archaeology, anthropology, and other fields* (pp. 58–70). Bowling Green, OH: Bowling Green State University Popular Press.

Sklar, S. (n.d.). *What is Khoomei?* Retrieved 7 June 2007 from http://www.atch.org/khoomei/wahtis.html.

Slyomovics, S. (1991). To put one's finger in the bleeding wound: Palestinian theatre under Israeli censorship. *Drama Review* 35(2): 18–37.

Soong, R. (2001). *The phenomenon of Yo Soy Betty la fea.* Retrieved 15 April 2007 from http://www.zonalatina.com/Zldata185.htm.

Sozanski, E.J. (2007, April 22). The Philadelphia Inquirer art column: Most certainly folk art. *Philadelphia Inquirer.* Retrieved 9 May 2007 from http://infotrac-college.thomsonlearning.com/itw/infomark/880/320/1145362w17/purl=rc1_WAD_0_cj162416842&dyn=22!ar_fmt?sw_aep=olr_wad.

Spalding, A.G. (1991). *Baseball: America's national game.* San Francisco, CA: Halo Books.

Spitulnik, D. (1993). Anthropology and mass media. Annual Review Anthropology 22:293-315. Retrieved 20 October 2008 from http://www.annualreviews.org/aronline.

Spitulnik, D. (2002). Mobile machines and fluid audiences: Rethinking reception through Zambian radio culture. In F. Ginsberg, L. Abu-Lughod, & B. Larkin (Eds.), *Media worlds: Anthropology on new terrain* (pp. 337–54). Berkeley, CA: University of California Press.

Stapley, K. (2000). Mizwid: An urban music with rural roots. *Journal of Ethnic and Migration Studies* 32(2): 243–56.

Starrett, G. (1999). Review of *Mass culture and modernism in Egypt. American Ethnologist* 26(2): 503–04.

Stastna, K. (2007, April 15). Muslim girl barred from tourney vows to wear *hijab. National Post.* Retrieved 9 May 2007 from http://www.canada.com/nationalpost/news/story.html?id=5b5dd9af-65b7-4e79-a300-5ac244f0c232&k=0.

Steinkuehler, C., & Williams, D. (2006). Where everybody knows your (screen) name: Online games as "third places." *Journal of Computer-Mediated Communication* 11(4): 1.

Stevenson, T.B., & Alaug, A.K. (2000). Football in newly united Yemen: Rituals of equity, identity, and state formation. *Journal of Anthropological Research* 56(4): 453–75.

Stock, J. (1996). *World sound matters: Teacher's manual.* London: Schott Educational Publications.

Stokes, M. (1992). *The Arabesk debate: Music and musicians in modern Turkey.* Oxford: Oxford University Press.

Stokes, M. (2006). Special issue introduction. *Journal of Musical Anthropology of the Mediterranean* 11. Retrieved 13 March 2007 from http://www.levi.provincia.venezia.it/ma/index/number11/potuoglu/pot_o.htm.

Strelitz, L. (2001). Where the global meets the local: Media studies and the myth of cultural homogenization. *Transnational Broadcast Studies* 6. American University of Cairo. Retrieved 17 June 2007 from http://www.tbsjournal.com/Archives/Spring01/strelitz2.html.

Stroeken, K. (2002). Why "the world" loves watching football (and "the Americans" don't). *Anthropology Today* 18(3): 9–13.

Subrahmanyam, K., Greenfield, P.M., & Tynes, B. (2004). Constructing sexuality and identity in an online teen chat room. *Applied Developmental Psychology* 25: 651–66.

147

Szwed, J. (2005). *Crossovers: Essays on race, music, and American culture.* Philadelphia, PA: University of Pennsylvania Press.

Szwed, J. F. (1970). Afro-American musical adaptation. In N.E. Whitten & J.F. Szwed (Eds.), *Afro-American Anthropology: Contemporary perspectives* (pp. 219–28). New York: Free Press.

Taft, M. (2009). The mock wedding: Folk drama in the prairie provinces. In W. Haviland, S. Fedorak, & R. Lee, *Cultural Anthropology,* 3rd Ed. (pp. 373–76). Toronto: Nelson Education Ltd.

Tanenbaum, D. (2004, July 29). *Is tattoo taboo?* University of Wisconsin. Retrieved 16 May 2007 from http://whyfiles.org/206tattoo/2.html.

Tardieu, J. (2000). *Fear of US pop culture dominance drives anti-globalization sentiment.* Retrieved 26 June 2007 from http://www/ksg.harvard.edu/citizen/07feb00/tardo207.html.

Taylor, C.S. (2003). Introductory editorial: Understanding youth culture. *Online Journal of Urban Youth Culture.* Retrieved 3 August 2007 from http://www.juyc.org/current/0302/taylor.html.

The AIDS Memorial Quilt (n.d.). *The Names Project Foundation.* Retrieved 17 November 2005 from http://www.aidsquilt.org/about.htm.

The Economist. (2004, April 24). Take me out to the ballgame: Sports anthropology. *Economist Newspaper.* Retrieved 2 May 2007 from http://infotrac-college.thomsonlearning.com/itw/infomark/213/924/487589w16/purl=rc1_WAD_0_A115807397&dyn=6!ar_fmt?sw_aep=olr_wad.

The Library of Congress. (2005). What is folk life? *The American Folklife Center.* Retrieved 19 November 2006 from http://www.loc.gov/folklife/whatisfolklife.html.

Toerpe, K.D. (2001). Jim Henson and the muppets. In R.B. Browne & P. Browne (Eds.), *The guide to United States popular culture* (pp. 441–42). Bowling Green, OH: Bowling Green State University Popular Press.

Tonkinson, R. (2002). *Spiritual prescription, social reality: Reflections on religious dynamics.* The Second Berndt Memorial Lecture. University of Western Australia. Retrieved 22 January 2005 from http://www.anthropology.arts.uwa.edu.aru/_data/page/27090/tonkinson_2002.pdf.

Tostanoski, H. (n.d.). *Pysanky.* Retrieved 6 December 2006 at http://tostanoski.com/pysanky.html.

Traphagen, J.W., & Brown, K. (2002). Fast food and intergenerational commensality in Japan: New Styles and old patterns. *Ethnology* 41(2): 119–34.

148

Turino, T. (2007). *The anthropology of music.* Retrieved 28 June 2007 from http://science.jrank.org/pages/0332/Music-Anthropology-Anthropology-Music.html.

Turk, I. (2003, November). *Neanderthal flute.* Slovenia Government Communications Office. Retrieved 5 June 2007 from http://www.ukom.gov.si/eng/slovenia/background-information/neanderthal-flute/.

Turner, V. (1986). *The anthropology of performance.* New York: PAJ Publications.

Underhill, P. (2004). *Call of the mall.* New York: Simon & Schuster.

Van Gennep, A. (1942). *Le folklore de l'Auvergne et du Velay.* Paris: Editions A. et J. Picard et Cie.

Van Gennep, A. (1946). *Manuel de folklore français contemporain.* Vol. 1, *Du berceau à la tombe.* Paris: Editions A. et J. Picard et Cie.

Verardi, B. (2000). I do? Northern New York's Mock Wedding. *The Journal of New York Folklore* 26 (Fall-Winter). Retrieved 17 February 2007 from http://www.nyfolklore.org/pubs/voicjl/mock.html.

Vianna, H. (1999). *The mystery of samba: Popular music and national identity in Brazil.* John Charles Chasteen, ed. & trans. Chapel Hill, NC: University of North Carolina Press.

Ward, K.J. (1999). Cyber-ethnography and the emergence of the virtually new community. *Journal of Information Technology* 14(1): 52–90.

Warner W. (1990, Winter). The resistance to popular culture. *American Literary History* 2(4): 726–42.

Weiner, A. (1988). *The Trobrianders of Papua New Guinea.* New York: Holt, Rinehart, & Winston.

Wellman, B., Quan-Haase, A., Boase, J., Chen, W., Hampton, K., de Diaz, I., & Miyata, K. (2003). The social affordances of the internet for networked individualism. *Journal of Computer-Mediated Communications* 8(3). Retrieved 25 September 2006 from http://jcmc.indiana.edu/vol8/issue3/wellman.html.

Wheeler, D.L. (2003). The internet and youth subculture in Kuwait. *Journal of Computer Mediated Communication.* Retrieved 14 November 2006 from http://jcmc.indiana.edu/vol8/issue2/wheeler.html.

Whitaker, J. (2001). Ethnic foods. In R.B. Browne & P. Browne (Eds.), *The guide to United States popular culture* (pp. 269–70). Bowling Green, OH: Bowling Green State University Popular Press.

Wilk, R.R. (1999). Real Belizean food: Building local identity in the transnational Caribbean. *American Anthropologist*, New Series 101(2): 244–55.

Williams, B. (1984). Why migrant women feed their husbands tamales: Foodways as a basis for a revisionist view of Tejano family life. In L. Keller-Brown & K. Mussel (Eds.), *Ethnic and regional foodways in the United States: The performance of group identity* (p. 113–26). Knoxville, TN: University of Tennessee.

Williams, C.T. (2001). Soap operas. In R.B. Browne & P. Browne (Eds.), *The guide to United States popular culture* (pp. 752–54). Bowling Green, OH: Bowling Green State University Popular Press.

Wilson, S.M., & Peterson, C. (2002). The anthropology of online communities. *Annual Review of Anthropology* 31: 449–67.

World Wide Quilting Page. (2006, May 18). Retrieved 6 September 2006 from http://www.quilt.com/.

Yinger, J.M. (1977). Presidential address: Countercultures and social change. *American Sociological Review* 42(6): 833–53.

Young, W. (1994). The body tamed: Tying and tattooing among the Rashaayda Bedouin. In I.N. Sault (Ed.), *Many mirrors: Body image and social relations* (pp. 58–75). New Brunswick, NJ: Rutgers University Press.

Yurdadon, E. (2003, Summer). Sport in Turkey: the pre-Islamic period. *The United States Sport Journal* 6(3). Retrieved 2 May 2007 from http:// www.thesportjournal.org/ 2003Journal/Vol6-No3/turkey.asp.

INDEX

152

154

155

G

gamer communities. *See* online gaming

gangs in Los Angeles, 61

Gans, Herbert, xv

garage sales, 3

gathering and celebration. *See also*
  food; sports; wedding rituals and
  ceremonies
  anthropology of, 82–83
  music in, 38

gathering places. *See also* community;
  virtual communities
  characteristics, 80–81
  coffee houses, 81
  definition, 116
  lacking in North American cities, 81
  third places, 80–81

gay and lesbian cafés, 49, 51, 55–59

gays or lesbians, 5
  on Brazilian television, 32

gender, 3, 15–16, 22, 73
  definition, 117
  female oppression, 17
  identity based on, xii
  performance theory and, 18
  role in body painting, 73

gender boundaries, 52–53

gender equality, 5, 8, 12, 31–32

gender gap (digital), 50

gender roles, 117
  defined through food, 82, 84, 90
  duality of prairie farm wife's gender
  roles, 19, 107–8

gender stereotypes, 8

gender stratification, 117
  in sports, 83, 100–101

Ghanian concert parties and paintings,
  xiii, 15, 19–22
  accessibility, 19
  concert plays, 20–22
  engagement between audience and
  performers, 19
  hybrid imagery, 19–20

ghinnáwa (little songs of the Awlad'Ali
  Bedouin), 41

Gilbert, Michelle, 15, 20, 22

Giroux, Henry, 79

global youth culture, xiii, 13, 117. *See also*
  youth
  cultural imperialism and, 111

globalization, 11, 117
  blurring of boundaries between high
  and low culture, 7, 14
  broadcasting of American popular
  culture, 10
  homogenization of local popular
  culture, 2, 10
  hybridization of popular culture, 4
  threat to indigenous cultures, xiii
  threat to local popular culture, xii,
  2, 4, 10
  through multinational corporations,
  111

globalization theories, 45, 47

glocalization, 51, 103, 117

Good Morning America, 110

"Gorbi" doll, 66

graffiti (or street art), xiii, 61, 67–71, 117
  audiences, 67, 70
  circumvention of censorship, 69
  considered vandalism, 67
  cultural resistance through, xiv, 67
  evolved from gang-related activities,
  67–68
  growing acceptance, 67
  Palestinian, xiv, 64, 69–70
  Rio de Janeiro, 64, 68–69
  rite of passage, 70
  social complexities in, 64
  street culture, youth subcultures, and
  artistic communities, 67
  Toronto, 64, 68–69

graffiti artists, 67
  encoding of graffiti, 61
  motivation, 68

graffiti tags, 68–69

Grandmaster Flash, 42
Grey's Anatomy (2005), 8

H

haiku poems, 55
Hamdiyya (character in *Hilmiyya Nights*), 34
hand-picked tattoos, 77
Hansen, Karen T., 84
Harvest of Love, 36
Have Faith in God (play), 20
hegemony, 100. *See also* cultural imperialism
    definition, 117
Hendrix, Jimi, 16
Henson, Jim, 28
high culture, 4, 6–7, 89
    and low culture distinction, 14
highlife music, 20
hijab, 17
    in sports, 101
    used as symbol of modernity, 18, 35
Hilmiyya Nights, 34, 36
hip hop culture, 38–39, 43–44. *See also* rap music
    about identity and self-assertion, 43
    activism, 47
    celebration of black culture, 47
    clothing, 46
    conspicuous consumption, 46–47
    definition, 117
    distinctive language, attitude, and lifestyle, 42, 47
    diversity (multiple voices), 46
    graffiti, 61, 68
    hustling and consumerism, 45, 47
    imagery, 43
    major countercultural force, 42
    multiple meanings, 43
    political protest, 41
hip hop movement in Cuba. *See* Afro-Cuban hip hop culture and rap music

hippies, 5, 75
Hmong textiles from Laos, 64, 67
Ho Chi Minh City, 85
holism, 16–17, 118
homogenization, xiii, 4, 11, 13, 24. *See also* cultural imperialism; hybridization
    definition, 118
    overstated, 12, 29, 90
homosexuality, 5, 32. *See also* gay and lesbian cafés
Hong Kong
    use of television (to strengthen cultural identity), 30
Howard, P.E.N., 49, 51–53
Huichol yarn paintings, 64–65
hybridization of popular culture, 4, 11, 40, 111, 118. *See also* homogenization
    hip hop graffiti, 61

I

identity, 16, 22, 118
    based on elements of popular culture, 4, 15
    based on gender, ethnicity, or class, xii
    defined through food, 90
    hip hop culture and rap, 43
    "mobilization of identity," 30
identity marker, 118
identity politics, 83
IM (Instant Messaging), 51–52
imagery, 19–20, 78
    definition, 118
Indigenous cultures, xiii
    Mayan people of Guatemala, 28–29
    popular culture and, 9
    tattoos, 74
    youth craving for Western goods, 9
Indigenous folk art and crafts, 10–11
Indigenous peoples
    definition, 118
    use of media to further political and cultural aims, 8, 29–30, 51

Leningrad Institute of Archaeology, 66

Lentz, Carola, 17

Lesbian Café, 51, 56, 59

lesbian cafés (LCs), 49, 55–57
   code of behaviour, 58
   participants, 58

linguistics, xiii

Listin Dairo, 98, 100

Llamosas, Juan, 67

local popular culture, 9, 19
   pressure from outside forces, 2, 10, 23, 111
   selectivity in adopting elements of other culture, 12, 111
   television's impact on, 27, 29, 36

Los Paisanos, 44

Lost, 36

M

Madonna, 11

magico-realist attitude, 94

Mahon, Maureen, 16

males. *See* men

Mardu Aborigines of Australia
   youth craving for Western goods, 9

marriage, 73. *See also* wedding rituals and ceremonies
   definition, 118
   joining of two families, 103–5
   socio-cultural functions, 103

mass culture theory, 4

mass media. *See* media (or mass media)

matryoshka. See Russian nesting dolls

Mayan people of Guatemala
   television's impact on, 28–29

McDonalds, 11, 86–87
   cultural icon, 92, 112

media (or mass media), xiii, xiv, 23–59.
   See also Internet; television
   agent of change, 23
   biased reports on graffiti, 68
   consumer manipulation, 9
   damaging effects, 10

definition, 118

escapist nature, 8

homogenization of non-Western popular culture, xiii

multiple meanings, 18

stereotyping, 8

supporting Dominican nationalism, 100

used to document traditional activities, 30

Mediascape, 59

melodrama serials, 30. *See also* Egyptian melodramatic serials; soap operas
   difficult social issues, 32

men. *See also* gender
   as soap opera viewers, 30
   status from barbecuing skills, 91–92

Mexican Americans, 5

Mexico
   baseball, 98

microcultures, 4, 118

MICROMUSE, 54

milaya, 17–18

Miller, Daniel, 5, 17

Miller, Laura, 59

mingei folk craft movement in Japan, 61

Mintz, S.W., 86, 88, 92

mizwid (Tunisian rap music), 41

mmotia, 19

"mobilization of identity," 30

mock weddings, xiii, xv, 83, 118
   conflicting or dual gender roles, 19, 106, 108
   cross-dressing, 106
   opportunity to socialize, 108
   production of, 107
   secular celebration, 108
   sexual innuendoes, 107

modernity, 18, 24, 36
   definition, 118

modernization, 4, 118
   threat to local popular culture, xii

Moeran, Brian, 61

160

162

la rôtie, xv, 83–84, 89
    chocolate and champagne, 88, 110
    many meanings, 88
    need for scholarly objectivity, 90
    reinforcement of local identity, 92
    rite of passage into married life, 88
    symbolic body fluids, 88
The Running Man (1987), 28
Russian nesting dolls, 63, 65–66

S

Sainte-Marie, Buffy, 7
SBS (rap group), 43, 45
"scratchers" (tattooist), 78
segregation, 99, 101, 120
semi-professional tattooing, 77
senior-ml, 55, 59
serial television programs.
    See Egyptian melodramatic
    serials; melodrama serials;
    soap operas; *telenovelas* in
    Latin America
Sesame Street, 28
sexism, 42. *See also* gender
sexuality, 22, 28, 107
    addressed in song, 41
    chat rooms, 52, 57
    performance theory and, 18
    "promiscuity," 96
shaabi (working-class music) from Egypt
    and Morocco, 38
shopping malls, 6
shopping online, 49, 52
Silverstone, Alicia, 74
"soap gossip," 32
soap operas, xiv, 12. *See also* Egyptian
    melodramatic serials; melodrama
    serials; *telenovelas* in Latin America
    breaking of social barriers, 31
    "Cinderella" storyline, 31
    disparaged, 31–32
    fans, 30–31
    popularity, 31–32, 37

social bonding and, 32
social solidarity from, 32
themes, 30
soccer. *See* football
social solidarity, 3, 32, 36
    definition, 120
social tolerance, 5
socializing, xii, xiv, 84. *See also*
    community; gathering and
    celebration; gathering places
    online, 25, 49
    through sports, 94–95
socializing/socialization
    definition, 120
socio-cultural anthropology, 15
Soviet Union (breakup), 44
    rock music and, 5
Spalding, A.G., 98
Spitulnik, Debra, 23
sports, 82–83, 93–102
    agent of cultural imperialism, xv,
        83, 94
    chance elements in, 94, 102
    cultural resistance through, xv, 83, 94
    embedded with male imagery, 101
    equality in, 100–101
    ethnic identities through, 96
    expression of nationalism, 93–94,
        96, 100
    forum for promoting socio-political
        messages, 98
    group identity through, 94
    multiple meanings, 94–100
    power to counteract American
        cultural hegemony, 100
    public performances or spectacles, 93
    racial and ethnic barriers, 101
    reflect socio-political and religious
        atmosphere, 95
    ritual, 83–84, 94, 96–98
    social bonding through, 94–95
    symbolism of, 93
    traditional, 94–95

163

Chinese, 3, 11, 111
cross-cultural approaches, 83
hybridity, 103
Japanese, 103
mock weddings, xiii, xv, 19, 83, 106, 118
as performative spectacles, 103
la rôtie, xv, 83–84, 88–90, 92, 110
Trobriander wedding rituals, 103
wedding dresses, 11, 103–4
wedding songs, 40
West Indians
hip hop culture and rap music, 41–42
Western popular culture, 4. *See also* cultural imperialism
blamed for spread of fast food, 87–88, 92
impact on youth in other cultures, 9, 111
Internet and, 50
mass marketing in other cultures, 9, 111–12
negative effect on local cultures, 11, 13
Western television programming
impact on local popular culture, 27
white wedding gowns, 11, 103–4
Whitehead, Neil, 62
Will and Grace (1998), 5
Williams, Raymond, 14
Wodaabes people
gerewol courting ritual, 73
women. *See also* Egyptian women; gender; lesbian cafés (LCs)
empowerment from food preparation, 90, 92
Kuwaiti, 53

tattoos as symbol of new independence, 75–76
work songs, 41
World Cup, 93
wycinanki paper cuts from Poland, 64

Y

yarn paintings of the Huichol people, 64–65
Yiddish music, 38
Yo Soy Betty La Fea, 32
youth, 2
access to music and video technology, 39
African-American, 44
Afro-Cuban, 44
body adornment, 79
consumer brand shopping in Egypt, 10
craving for Western goods, 9
Egyptian television and, 29
Inuit, 51
receptiveness to foreign influences, 11, 13
use of chat rooms (dating), 52
warung food stalls, 86
youth culture, 5–6, 11, 13, 50, 67, 111, 117.
See also hip hop culture; rap music
popular music and, 39
Puerto Rican, 68
youth subcultures, 53, 67

Z

Zairian *soukous*, 38
Zulu Nation, 42